THE GIFT OF *Encouragement*

How to be a Warm Shoulder in a Cold World

by Gloria Chisholm

Aglow Publications

A Ministry of Women's Aglow Fellowship, Int'l.
P.O. Box 1548
Lynnwood, WA 98046-1558
USA

Cover design by David Marty

ISBN 0-932305-30-X

To
Joanne, Iris, Sharon, and Sally
who remained

To
Barbara and Elaine
who restored

Contents

Contents

Introduction

What is it that causes me to put one foot in front of the other? What motivates me, propels me on in the face of impossible difficulties and hardships? Why do I keep trying when everything inside screams out "Failure"?

Why do I "press on toward the goal to win the prize for which God has called me heavenward in Christ Jesus" (Phil. 3:14)? Because certain people believe in me and commit time, energy, and prayer to see that I make it.

When I kick and scream and fight love off, they hold me.

When I run away, they follow.

When I fall, they help me up, brush me off, and gently nudge me onward.

They are my encouragers, enabled and gifted by God, sent on a mission, grafted into my life for the purpose of building me up in my innerself, loving me in my weaknesses, affirming me in my strengths.

Each of us can make a difference in one another's lives. We build up or tear down, we give life or stifle it. Whether it's a conscious mental effort or not, we either bring healing or add to a person's hurt.

This book was born during the most painful time of my life. I know what it's like to be crushed by "the truth spoken in love." I've been misunderstood by those who appointed themselves my personal motive inspectors. I've received letters of "encouragement" from those who must be descendants of "Job's comforters." I've grieved over those who walked away at the point of my greatest need.

Yet, more important than all that, a few stuck around. They stayed through my anger, my indifference, and my utter and total despair. Through their influence on my life, I learned loyalty and endurance, and I came to understand the tenacious kind of love God has for us.

Introduction

They took me as far as they could.

At that point God activated His restoration crew. And I'm indebted to them for the hours they've given me—on the phone, in the car, in restaurants, in their homes, and most of all in prayer. They have ushered me into the awesome presence of a God I've served for many years, yet had never known. Because of their response to my need, I now serve a God who I know loves me unconditionally and forgives me when I blow it. Now, instead of visions of a perpetual frown, I see and feel His arms stretched out, always waiting, always welcoming.

These two encouragers have altered my life—eternally.

We can only encourage one another if we ourselves have been encouraged: "Freely you have received, freely give" (Matt. 10:8). I take this opportunity to give to you that which I've been freely given.

May I bestow on you: hope in God, peace in circumstances, belief in one another. As you read the following pages, may you receive healing for yesterday's hurts, courage for today's tasks, and strength to face tomorrow.

With God's help you can do it; you can make it. He expresses His help through someone's arms to hold you, someone's tears mixed with yours, someone's willingness to stay by your side even when you're not being nice.

Have you ever been encouraged? Have you freely received? For although I want you to receive from this book, I will have failed in my purpose if you don't take its principles and give to the others in your life.

Always hopeful, others look to us for a response. In desperation, they wait—longing for that response to be a positive one, yearning for acceptance, unconditional love. Don't let them down. Be the one who stays after everyone else has gone.

Encourage one another.

1

...

What is Encouragement?

My friend Donna sat across the table from me and traced the design on her half-empty coffee cup with her index finger. Her eyes met mine soberly as she spoke: "The best part of the retreat was when we were asked to divide up into small groups to encourage each other."

"Oh? What made that so special to you?"

"I needed it so badly. We've been working with the kids in our church for two years now, and the parents are always quick to come to us when we do something wrong. I needed to hear what I was doing right." She leaned back in her chair, tears glistening in her eyes. "I hung on to every word. I knew I wouldn't hear that kind of encouragement again for at least another six months, maybe not until the next retreat."

I left Donna's house that day, saddened by her words,

carrying them like huge boulders inside my heart.

Six months? Was she serious? Donna and her husband served their church faithfully, nurturing the youth. They gave of themselves until they were ready to drop, leading youth meetings, retreats, checking on absentees, facilitating summer projects.

Yet I'd sensed no bitterness in her voice, only gratitude for the few words of encouragement she had received at the retreat.

Six months? Really? This from the church of Jesus Christ, a living organism that reflects the very heart of God, the Author of encouragement?

I found this hard to accept, yet because of my own heavy involvement in the church I knew it was sadly true. Many times after completing a project I struggle with feelings of inadequacy, failure, a poor self-image. And, when none of my friends or acquaintances assure me otherwise, I assume that my self-evaluation has been quite accurate and that my feelings are justified—I really *have* blown it.

Occasionally I have mustered up the courage to ask someone if my performance was really that bad.

"What? You did great! Everyone I've talked to has said what a fantastic job you did!"

How come no one told *me?*

And let us consider how we may spur one another on toward love and good deeds. Let us not give up meeting together, as some are in the habit of doing, but let us encourage one another—and all the more as you see the Day is approaching.

Hebrews 10:24–25

What is the author of Hebrews admonishing us to do? What does it mean to encourage? One dictionary defines the word *encourage* as "to inspire with courage, hope, or confidence; to embolden or hearten." As the exhortation in verse 24 implies, to encourage is "to spur one another on toward love and good deeds."

Encouragement can and does take many forms. Let's examine some of them closely and see exactly how the concept of building others up is implemented in practical day-to-day living.

ENCOURAGEMENT IS . . . A STRONG ARM

Times come to all of us when we need to lean on others for support. At times I have leaned so strenuously on my friends that I'm sure I must have squashed them as flat as a Frisbee.

How do we provide that strong arm that others so desperately need in their times of discouragement? Only as we lean on the Lord can we supply a sturdy support for someone else. I realize that "Lean on the Lord" has become a trite cliché in this day of self-help books like *I'm OK—You're OK* and *The Cinderella Complex*. Why lean on a Higher Power when we're okay?

The sober truth is that without the Lord we're not okay. Human compassion is an ailing commodity supplying only temporary relief to the hurting. It has no enduring substance, no solution to bring permanent healing. My arm alone will not bring healing to you, but together—as our arms are tucked into the Lord's arm—hope becomes a reality and wholeness a very real probability.

Galatians 6:2 admonishes us to "carry each other's burdens." This is impossible in our own strength, and if we attempt it, our own weakness may actually hinder those who try to lean on us. Since an arm can't talk, it offers no advice. It is simply there to support. Likewise, the strong arm of encouragement supports those who for one reason or another are finding it difficult bearing up under the loads they are carrying.

In essence, encouragement says, "I'm here if and when you need me."

ENCOURAGEMENT IS . . . A LOUD CHEER

When I lay in the delivery room of the hospital birthing my fourth child, this absolutely crazy staff of nurses was on duty. Of my five deliveries at the same hospital, this one manifests itself vividly in my memory as one of the most thrilling events in my life.

These zany nurses cheered loudly. They clapped. Rousing choruses of "You can do it!" "All right!" "You're doing just great!" reverberated against the walls and ceiling of the brightly lit delivery room. One nurse's supportive hands on my back felt warm and comforting. Another held my hand tightly.

I don't know where they are now, but I'll never forget their encouragement as my attention was redirected from the intense pain of the moment to the necessity of concentrating my energy on delivering my baby. I remember thinking, "Yeah, I can do it. They believe I can."

Encouragement does not mean sitting by stoically while someone announces an answer to prayer, a raise in salary, or even a final victory in potty-training a child.

Encouragement responds. In fact, encouragement cheers loud and long.

I have two kinds of friends—those I call when something good happens to me . . . and those I don't. New friends fall from the I-do-call category into the I-don't-call classification when they respond with: "Oh" or "That's nice" or "Really? What else has been happening?"

From the I-do-call friends I receive various responses—anything from a loud shriek to "Oh, I'm so proud of you! I knew you could do it!" During an especially low period, a hearty cheer will often be just what I need to jar me from my state of lassitude.

In the Christian race we function in two roles: (1) as runners, and (2) as cheerleaders. When we're given the opportunity to cheer, let's not sit idly by and mumble, "Oh, yes, how nice."

ENCOURAGEMENT IS . . . A WARM HAND

When we're immobilized by fear, we have no strength left to reach out when we're in the dark, many times all we need is for someone to extend a hand to us and say, "I'll walk with you. Take my hand and we'll travel this road together." We need someone who will not release us no matter how much we hang back, drag our feet, or attempt to free ourselves from their warm but firm handclasp.

Once, during a time of despair, I made a feeble attempt to push all of my close friends out of my life, pleading for them to leave me alone, but my friend Iris tenaciously refused to back off: "You can tell me to leave, to move away, to back off, to never come back . . . it doesn't matter. I'm not budging . . . because I love you too much to let you go."

By this time I was sobbing. "Promise?" I whimpered.

"Promise."

I wanted her to go because I felt I was such a burden to her right then. Yet, if she had listened to me, I would have been furious. I'm sure my reaction would have been, "I tell her to flake off and she does! What kind of a friend is that?"

But she stayed. Our hands remained locked together . . . and so did our hearts.

Offering a hand to someone involves a huge commitment of time and a sacrifice of personal freedom. When we join hands with another, we take on ourselves the responsibility to stay and stay—and stay some more. Our hands are emblematic of the hands of Jesus Christ. As Christ reached out to others so must we: "Immediately Jesus reached out his hand and caught him" (Matt. 14:31). "Filled with compassion, Jesus reached out his hand and touched the man" (Mark 1:41).

Someone somewhere waits for your hand to reach out to them. They need a warm hand of encouragement to grab hold of, to hang on to.

ENCOURAGEMENT IS . . . A GENTLE PROD

Have you ever needed a nudge? Have you ever simply needed someone to say, "Oh, c'mon! You can do it."

I have. In fact, I need that kind of prodding almost daily.

A gentle prod like "Oh, c'mon" motivates, pushes, and moves others ever so gradually.

"I can't teach a Bible study. I've never done it before. No way."

"Oh, c'mon, you can too. You've taught Sunday school and I've heard you share a number of times at our home group. You're an excellent communicator."

"Me? You really think so? Well, maybe I could try. . . ."

It took me several weeks to convince a friend of mine that she could lead worship at our monthly women's group meeting. She had already been leading in worship at the weekly Bible study, and doing a beautiful job. All the women in the group attested to it.

Because four times as many women would be at the monthly meeting and the setting was more formal, she was sure she couldn't pull it off. Fear consumed her.

Yet I continued to prod—gently. "Kelly, I know you can do it. You're so sensitive to the Holy Spirit, always leaving room for Him to move. Worship flows so smoothly when you lead it."

14

Every time we connected, I reminded her that the Lord wanted to use her in a mighty way in the future, but she needed to take this step first. And each time she reminded me, not quite so gently, that no way could she get up in front of all those women.

The whole situation culminated in a sermon our pastor preached a week before the meeting. "Fear and timidity are not of God," he said. "Those of you who are afraid to speak or sing in front of people need to get over it and the only way to get over it is to face it and do what you fear." He continued with illustrations and Scripture to confirm his point.

I moved through various contortions (not a spiritual way to act in church, I admit), trying to catch Kelly's eye, but she was intent on what the pastor was saying.

Immediately after the prayer of dismissal, I about broke my neck leaping over chairs to grab her before she escaped.

She saw me coming. "Oh, no. I was hoping to get out of here before I ran into you. Okay, I'll do it, I'll do it."

She did and God honored her obedience. We heard many times over what the Lord did through the worship that Kelly led at that month's meeting.

A gentle prod—not necessarily the easiest way to encourage, but sometimes the most effective.

ENCOURAGEMENT IS . . .
AN UNDERSTANDING SMILE

Of all the men who ever lived, Jesus Christ had to be the most misunderstood. No one, not even those in His close inner circle, grasped the perfect plan of the Father who sent His Son to earth to die. They expected Jesus to establish His kingdom on earth. (See John 6:14–15.) That lack of understanding must have hurt.

Oh, for someone to understand! For someone to smile

my direction in a tense moment.

One Sunday before church a friend approached me and confided in me something she had told no one else, not even her husband. In a moment of extreme frustration, she had committed an act the ramifications of which were far-reaching. Her whole future would be altered, and certainly her marriage now hung in the balance.

I hugged her and had time only to ask a question or two before our pastor began the service. Then I excused myself by saying, "I'd better go sit down now."

She gasped. "After what I just told you, all you have to say is you'd better go sit down?"

What else could I do at the moment? As I made my way to a seat, I realized she already regretted her impulsive confession and needed to know I still loved her. Since I could see her easily from where I sat, periodically throughout the service (whenever I could get her atttention), I simply smiled in understanding, letting her know I did not stand in judgment over her. She told me later how much it meant to her that I did that.

Have you ever been sharing your thoughts on a very personal level in a roomful of people and suddenly realize that half the group is nodding and smiling in understanding? They've been there, too. They know and feel what you're verbalizing. Of course, if you're not used to sharing your inner feelings, let me caution you . . . that type of response doesn't always happen. Sometimes you encounter hostile looks or signs of embarrassment.

I've seen all kinds because I'm a gut-spiller. Not that I ever plan it that way. I just open my mouth and it gushes out—all of it. I'm often accused of saying aloud what everyone else is thinking but won't admit. Oh, well, that's my cross to bear.

So you can see why I need lots of understanding smiles;

it works wonders to know I'm not the only one who has ever felt like leaving my family and running away to Saudi Arabia—without even having prayed about it!

ENCOURAGEMENT IS . . . A KICK IN THE PANTS

All of us need that special person in our lives (I have a couple of them) who will give us a good kick when called for.

The only problem with this kind of encouragement is that it hurts and not many of us are willing to risk hurting our friends. We may spank our children for their ultimate good because we love them, but we pussyfoot around with our friends because we want them to like us. We're afraid that if we kick them, they might say, "Ouch! I don't think I need you after all."

Is it worth the risk to attempt to stop those you love from making a bad decision or to help them see that what they're doing can only lead to heartache? Possibly they'll thank you down the road. Possibly not—and that is one of the risks you take.

A kick from a friend (and it has to be a dear friend or I shrug it off) initially makes me angry. But given time, I can usually acknowledge that my friend was right and I need to reorder that area of my life.

Of course we can't stomp around, kicking everyone with our spiritual boots, trying to whip all of them into shape. However, occasions do arise when the Holy Spirit would say to us that the time for sweetness is over, that a certain person needs a swift kick in the pants, a rebuke.

You may feel that the word *encouragement* cannot be used in conjunction with a kick in the pants. Yet what is our definition of encouragement? *To spur one another on toward love and good deeds.* When a kick in the pants is sponsored by the Holy Spirit, it will bear fruit.

17

ENCOURAGEMENT IS . . . A LOVING EMBRACE

Loving embrace is a sophisticated term for a plain, old-fashioned hug. A hug is one of the very best means of encouragement because it states, "I love you—right now." And how many of us need to be loved right now? When words are inadequate, a hug reveals our deepest feelings for another person. It says, "I accept you, I love you, I support you, I believe in you, I stand with you."

I remember a particularly trying time in my life when I was hugged by a friend who seldom touched anyone. At least I'd never seen her hug anyone before. Yet in front of ten other people, she reached out and embraced me before she left my house one evening. It meant more to me than anything else she could have done because she acted spontaneously—from her heart. I needed her expression of love at that time. She sensed that and moved on the impulse.

"Please shut up and just hold me!" I sometimes want to scream at the church—the body of Christ. Yet they talk on . . . and on . . . and on, completely unaware that there may be something besides a sermon to minister to the hurts and sufferings of their brothers and sisters.

"Encourage me. Please, just hold me."

ENCOURAGEMENT IS . . . SILENCE

A sign hangs on my bulletin board that reads: THE DEEP-EST FEELING SHOWS ITSELF IN SILENCE.

What makes silence so encouraging? To begin with, silence *listens*. It's impossible to talk and listen at the same time. There are times to talk, but first we need to listen in order to be effective encouragers. Silence also *thinks:* "What can I do or say to bring hope into this situation?" In the stillness of the soul, the solution will be unveiled. Finally, silence *feels*. In quietness we can fully experience our emotions before we express them.

In being silent, we gain confidence in ourselves to speak only those words the Lord would have us speak to encourage someone. A person sharing innermost thoughts and feelings may reach a place where he or she is groping for the right words. If we jump in with a bunch of excess verbiage to fill up what we feel is an awkward silence, we'll absolutely murder the conversation. Silence doesn't have to be awkward. It is only if we make it so.

When we don't know what to say, silence is better than saying the wrong thing, for untimely words may discourage. In our desire to be encouragers, we need to remember that many times encouragement is primarily a matter of knowing when to keep our mouths shut.

ENCOURAGEMENT IS . . . A SOFT VOICE

Many methods of encouragement are nonverbal, but all in all, *words* of encouragement are what we use the most. Our words represent us—our feelings and our thoughts—to others. We do not always say things perfectly and the message may come out muddled and with various shades of meaning we never intended, but the spirit behind our words is what will make them precious to the hearer. That is not to minimize the actual content of what we say; we need to choose our words carefully, especially when someone is discouraged. But if we goof and say the wrong thing, God will minister grace to those we try to encourage.

"Judas and Silas . . . *said* much to encourage and strengthen the brothers" (Acts 15:32).

The awesome thing about our words is that people, at least those who know and respect us, tend to believe us when we speak. They even gain a perspective of who they are from what we say. With this kind of influence, we can make or break those we love. To be encouragers we must

19

be ever mindful of the power of our words, remembering to use a soft voice of encouragement

I want to be an encourager. Possibly my loftiest aspiration is to give my life to recognizing the good in others and, by expressing my heart to them, motivating them to be all that God intends for them to be. I want to be a part of seeing God's plan fulfilled in those I love by believing in them, expecting the best from them, and supporting them to that end.

On the foundation of encouragement lies the cornerstone of the emotional and spiritual health of the body of Christ. Do you want to be part of what God is doing in His church?

TIME TO CONSIDER

1. When has encouragement been a loud cheer for you? Who has cheered you and why? Think of someone you can cheer. How will your cheering make a difference in that person's life?

2. How can you "spur others on toward love and good deeds" (Heb. 10:24)? Is confrontation often encouraging? How?

3. Is there anyone in your life right now who needs understanding from you? How can you show that person that you understand?

4. Why is silence often so encouraging? When is silence not encouraging? How can we encourage others quietly?

5. What does it mean to "carry each others' burdens"? As others lean on us for encouragement, how can we lean more on the Lord?

2

...

Does Anyone Care?

I love to encourage others for what it activates in them. I like to watch as they begin to believe in themselves and to develop confidence in their usefulness in the kingdom of God. I enjoy motivating them on to good deeds by my words. I've learned, however, that encouragement for its own sake is futile. As flowery and beautiful as it may emerge, if it lacks sincerity and truth, what I think of as encouragement may only be manipulation. Unless it comes from the core of my very being—unless I really care— encouragement is quickly reduced to exploitation. We must be constantly examining and reexamining our motives to make certain we're encouraging others for the right reasons.

What does it mean to be "real" and how do we know if we're being real or artificial? It's not always easy to make the distinction.

We are admonished in Scripture to examine ourselves (1 Cor. 11:28; 2 Cor. 13:5). By self-examination, we discover the person who lies under the superficial surface we present to the world. What do you personally feel? What do you truly think? Do you know? Or have you hitched a ride on the wings of your spouse, your friends, your church? Have you merely accepted their thoughts and ideas as your own?

In order to genuinely encourage others, our senses must be alive, our minds alert, and our hearts open as we observe those around us. We can't live in a vacuum and expect to be encouragers. We must think, feel, see, and hear.

THINK

Many people float around in a vacuous state, totally preoccupied with their own past or future, never thinking about anyone but themselves and whatever concerns them alone. Various degrees of vacuity exist, but more people than we realize subsist in this empty, selfish, and unthinking condition.

The vacuous person is characterized by such inane conversations (or monologues) as: "What did you do this weekend?" and—before you can answer—he or she continues with "*I* went to the fair [beach, mountains, rodeo, or whatever fits the occasion]." These people drift from conversation to conversation, be it on the phone or in person, never penetrating the surface of others' lives because they really *don't care*. Sadly, they cannot even imagine there being anything beneath the surface of anyone else's life because their minds are consumed with thoughts of "me, me, me."

As long as they remain in this state, they will never be encouragers—for the minds of encouragers must be occupied with thoughts of others and their needs. Paul exhorts us to look not only to our "own interests, but also to the interests of others" (Phil. 2:4).

What does all this have to do with being "real"? The key word is *caring*, and we cannot genuinely care enough about others to encourage them if we are never thinking about them.

How, then, does one move from egotism to an altruistic frame of mind? How can the way we think cause us to be encouragers?

1. *Realize that others are as important as you are.* Does the entire universe revolve around you? Do you think that everyone is sitting idle, anticipating the day you come back from your vacation so life can resume? Is your view on foreign affairs the only one? Do you really believe that the party cannot start until you step into the room?

If you were to die, I dare say the world would continue to rotate. Your co-workers, friends, and relatives may have the audacity to continue to function while you are on vacation. Someone may express an opposite view on foreign affairs. The party just might begin without you.

We stand equal in the sight of God.

2. *Know that others need your input.* Although you are not indispensable, you do make a considerable difference in your own world. You can change your thinking patterns if you begin to understand that your daily contacts with people are God's opportunities to use you. Can you believe that you can actually alter the course of a person's day for better or worse? And not only a day, but an entire lifetime? Believe me, you can make a permanent difference in someone's life.

It has happened to me numerous times. A friend once informed me that I was "walking in unforgiveness" (one of those encouraging but kick-in-the-pants friends I mentioned in chapter one). She was absolutely correct, and as her words passed through the filtering system of the Holy Spirit, they transformed my life.

We can choose either to erect a wall or build a bridge to every person we meet. We must carefully weigh each brick that we lay, ensuring that we are not building walls instead of bridges.

3. *Crystallize your thoughts.* If those precious (and seemingly at times not so precious) people whom God places in your life really need your encouragement, you want to have something worthwhile to say. First, you'll need to think through what it is you appreciate about them. Did you observe them as they performed an unselfish act? What part of their personality do you treasure the most? Have you seen them grow and mature in certain areas of their lives?

Someone once said to me, "We need you, Gloria."

Me? Foot-in-the-mouth, brash, unpredictable, crazy at times me? Someone needed *me?*

By "we," this friend made reference to a particular Bible study I had once attended regularly but had since dropped out of. In thinking about it, she'd apparently looked around the group and deduced for some unexplainable reason that they needed me. Whether they did or not in this case was irrelevant. The important thing was she *thought* they did— because she saw in me something she figured they needed. I wonder what wonderful quality it was! I should have asked her.

Anyway, as the thought entered her mind, she began indeed to feel that it was true. Thus, she could speak the thought aloud and be sincere in doing so. Our thoughts dictate our feelings.

FEEL

When we "feel" something, we experience it emotionally. We often hear so much about "walking by faith and not feelings" that we are afraid to identify our emotions, hesitant to place too much emphasis on them. Yet, Jesus was sorrowful (Matt. 26:37), compassionate (Mark 1:41), angry (Mark 3:5), loving (John 13:34), joyful (John 17:13), to name a few.

Emotions in themselves are not detrimental; it is how we act on our emotions that is crucial. If we are feeling compassion for someone, it doesn't do that person a lot of good if we only sit there and look sad. Compassion often moves us to the point of tears, which *show* how much we care. But godly compassion also produces action if there is anything at all that we can *do* to help alleviate the pain.

Feelings are an essential ingredient in the act of encouragement. They are the impetus through which we are able to share aloud what otherwise may have proceeded no further than our thoughts.

To get more in touch with your feelings try stopping at any point during the day to analyze them. Do this when you are with other people. How do you feel about Carolyn's new chartreuse dress? If it makes you sick, obviously this is not the area in which the Lord would use you to encourage Carolyn, for the paramount factor here should be sincerity and a positive attitude.

What do you feel about your pastor's sermons? He needs your encouragement. Out of a half-hour sermon, surely you can recall one point that ministered to you in a specific area of your life. Even if a sermon puts you to sleep, you're usually awake long enough to grasp at least one ray of truth.

Stepping back to examine your feelings will prevent you from speaking insincere words of adulation. Remember, ". . . a flattering mouth works ruin" (Prov. 26:28).

Can we always trust our feelings? Of course not. But do

you really believe Satan could ever be the one responsible for sponsoring positive feelings in our hearts toward those around us? When our motives are pure, we can trust the Lord with those emotions that impel us to move into others' lives with a word of encouragement.

SEE

In order to think any good thoughts, in order to experience any positive feelings toward others, we have to see people—really *see* them—and their needs.

Here is how I do this with my children: First I ask, "Lord, where does Grant need to be encouraged today? How can I make this a better day for him?" Then I watch him carefully, trying to be sensitive to his needs. If he seems angry, we might sit down and have a talk, discovering the solution together. If he seems lonely, I'll spend time with him playing a game or reading a book. If he seems sad, I try to make him laugh, or I might cry with him if I'm feeling sad, too.

That happened not long ago. He came into my office sobbing. "Mom, no one will play with me," he cried. "I don't have any friends. No one likes me."

"Oh, Grant, I know how you feel." I took him on my lap and began to rock him. "I feel the same way right now."

Together we cried. On any other occasion I would have tried to console him with positive words like: "It'll be okay." "Tomorrow they'll like you." "You don't need those kinds of friends anyway." But at that moment it wouldn't have been honest for me to say that. After we cried, we both felt better and played a game together.

Of course, tomorrow truly was better—they liked us again.

How can we develop super-vision, an eye for probing beyond the various façades others use to cover their true feelings? It helps to know people in depth. My close friends can see right through all of my masks. In fact, I don't even bother to put them on anymore when I'm with someone who knows me intimately.

With those we know less well, it's more difficult to see the real person and his or her needs. It takes more time, but if we're really looking—if we really care—eventually a crack in their façade will allow us to see their need and minister the healing balm of encouragement. Truly seeing others is fundamental to genuineness. Without it encouragement will be hollow as well as inaccurate.

I remember a friend who once prayed for me and, during the course of her prayer, thanked God for my humility. I appreciated her prayer, but I knew instantly that she had not been viewing me correctly. Had she been seeing me, not in a critical way but perceptively, she would have recognized that the area of growth needed in my life at that very time was a purging of pride. It did not take x-ray vision to see it either, just a pair of discerning eyes.

As you enter the sanctuary on Sunday, your office on Monday, the store on Wednesday, or wherever else your normal week takes you, begin to look beyond yourself and your immediate objective to the people around you. What do you sense that they need from you today? If you walk by Suzanne's desk intent only on your day's work instead of stopping to inquire as to her condition with an elementary "how's your life today?" you could miss the opportunity to encourage a heart whose life is not so great right now.

Too many of us do not really *see* other people. Instead we habitually look through them to the next item on our agenda. Our children cry out for us to *see* their needs. Our co-workers, each feeling like just one more cog in the wheel, silently scream, "Look at me! I'm a human being!" Our next-door neighbor entreats us: "Look into my eyes. I

27

need more from you today than a cup of coffee. I need your shoulder. Encourage me."

Let's not flatter each other with empty, hollow words, devoid of genuineness because we're too lazy, fearful, or preoccupied to recognize the needs of those dear ones who "clutter" our single-minded paths each day. Instead, let's take a minute from our busy schedules to stop and take a long, hard look at the person in front of us and—if there is a need—know that God can use us at this point in time to bring hope to a weary and discouraged life.

HEAR

"Would you please listen?" a wife pleads with her husband who is hiding behind the evening newspaper.

"I heard every word you said," the husband replies impatiently without laying down his paper. "I can repeat it verbatim."

He proceeds to echo his wife's words, but she's not satisfied. He has indeed heard her voice. He hasn't heard her heart.

We are admonished over and over in Scripture that "he who hath ears to hear, let him hear."

Why must we be reminded that listening is so important? Do not most people have ears? Why, then, do some not hear?

When someone tells you he or she loves you, that individual could be saying any (or all) of the following: "I accept you," "I commit myself to you," "I need you," "Let's go to bed," "I enjoy you," "I'm getting goose bumps!"—or one of many more. It's up to you, the recipient of that phrase, to decipher what is meant by "I love you."

Likewise, when a person who needs to be encouraged says to you, "I hurt," it could mean anything from "I stubbed my toe" to "I want to commit suicide." Again, it's up to you to hear what the heart is crying behind the words. Look, for example, at the following dialogue:

"I hurt."

"Oh? Well, don't cry. You'll be better soon."

"But I hurt."

"Okay then, here's a Band-Aid."

"Please. I hurt—bad."

"Hey, I've got problems of my own, you know."

"I can't stand the pain any longer."

"Sure you can. God's grace is sufficient. Just trust the Lord."

"Won't someone please listen?"

Too often we rely on easy answers and simple formulas. We take the easy way out by pushing off another's problems on the Lord so that we don't have to get personally involved. We do it with expressions like:

"I'll put you on my prayer list first thing."

"Read Philippians 4."

"The Lord is the One who meets all our needs. Isn't He wonderful?"

It can be a risky business to admit pain in the church today. So many ears are available, but so few of them are open. At least in the world, there's mutual understanding. Consider the following scenario:

"I hurt."

"Oh, yeah? You and me both. Let's hit the local pub" (where Joe the bartender listens and listens and listens some more).

How can we improve our capacity to hear?

1. *Listen to the tone of voice.* Does it crack, tremble, or fluctuate?

2. *Watch the facial expression.* Do you see anger, bitterness, sorrow, or self-pity?

29

3. *Ask provocative questions*. What specifically is wrong?

4. *Repeat aloud what you think you heard*. Do you really understand?

5. *Most important, care*.

If we truly care about other people, genuineness and sincerity won't even be an issue. Do I really care that your son is on drugs? Does it matter to me that you have no food in your cupboards? Does it make a difference to me that your marriage is crashing down around you?

How much do I care? How much do *you* care?

What can we do to help relieve one another's suffering? For that is both our responsibility and privilege as members together in the body of Christ.

Let us *care* for one another.

TIME TO CONSIDER

1. Do you feel you are a person who cares about others? What or who brings out your compassion?

2. How much of your day is spent thinking about yourself? How much is spent thinking of others? How can you nurture the habit of thinking about others more than you do yourself?

3. Why are feelings important in the act of encouraging others? How do you know which feelings to act on?

4. What are you doing to improve your vision when it comes to "seeing" the people in your life? How can you move beyond their facades to encourage them?

5. How can you hear beyond what others are saying to what they're not saying?

3

...

Dare to Step Out of Your World

The tendency in all of us is to go on our merry way through life, with our own concerns and problems foremost on our minds at any given moment. Granted, it's an effort, and a taxing one at that, to think about others when we have countless troubles of our own. So why bother?

(I wonder if God asked that question before He created mankind? I wonder if Jesus asked it in the Garden of Gethsemane as He faced crucifixion? And I wonder if the Holy Spirit asked it before the Day of Pentecost?)

The reasons for becoming an encourager are many, not the least of which is that we are commanded by God to "encourage one another." In this chapter we are going to look at what happens when we dare to move out of our own safe, little worlds to encourage others. And we'll see more clearly the answer to the question, "Why bother?" First let's look at what can happen to a tired, listless spirit when someone dares to be an encourager.

ENCOURAGEMENT . . . REFRESHES THE SPIRIT

Does your spirit ever get tired? Perhaps there are days when you think:

"I can't pray about this anymore."

"I'm not getting anything out of the Word lately."

"God, where are you?"

"Am I really a Christian? I don't feel like one."

At those weary times in my life, my prayers seem to bounce off a brick wall. I can't hear God, so I'm grateful for friends who will encourage me and take it upon themselves to hold me up before the throne of God until I'm strong again.

During one such occasion, a friend told me that whenever she prayed for specific guidance or direction for me, God would not give it to her. What she *did* hear God say was that I needed to trust Him for today, that tomorrow would take care of itself. Her eyes mirrored apprehension as she delivered this message and waited for my reaction.

Trust? Me, who had everything in my life scheduled weeks and months in advance? It was advice that was hard for me to swallow and my friend knew it, for she was only too aware of my organized lifestyle.

However, my ambivalence toward the future surprised even me. It was a huge test of faith for me to remain incognizant of tomorrow's blueprint, yet I simultaneously breathed a giant sigh of relief. For so long, tomorrow had seemed too insurmountable for me to face, but now I didn't have to worry about it. God's desire was that I trust Him— today. And I was fairly certain I could handle today.

My dear friend's words had brought encouragement that refreshed my spirit.

ENCOURAGEMENT ... REINFORCES WORTH

During moments of discouragement, our self-esteem often takes a nose dive. And we need to be reminded of who we are—a King's child, fearfully and wonderfully made. In times of failure or despondency, we may *feel* useless and lacking in purpose, but in God's eyes our value never wavers. Yet feelings are very real. That's why we need to be sensitive to reinforcing in one another that value that is resident in all of us—that we're all equally important to God.

Too frequently, however, it is not God's view of our personage that concerns us. Instead, it's our sense of worth to one another, which is why reading the Bible at these times does not always mitigate the situation. I know God thinks I'm terrific. It's you I'm wondering about. When I've botched up, I need to be reassured of your love immediately, if not sooner.

How easy it is to advise, "Now, now, it's not what I think that's important. It's what God thinks."

Oh, sure. That sounds high and noble, but I have to live with *you*. I have to look you in the eye. You can go ahead and tell me it doesn't matter, but if I feel that I've disappointed you, I won't be able to live with myself.

I remember once writing a note to two dear friends with whom I had really bungled a relationship. They were leaving for the beach, and I wrote: "I wish I could go to the beach with you and leave me here." I was that sick of myself.

Please tell me you still need me—now.

I'm significant and so are you, not because of what we do or fail to do for one another, but because of *who we are* to one another. I may have high expectations for you in an area in which you let me down. But that won't alter my feelings for you; you're still the same person you were before the mess.

So, to reinforce your sense of self-worth, it's important for me to underscore once again those precious qualities in you that drew us together in the beginning.

I love you because you are. . . .

ENCOURAGEMENT . . . RESTORES JOY

We are led to believe that when we become children of God, the attribute of joy enters into our hearts, never to depart. While it's true that nothing or nobody can rob us of joy, we can allow circumstances to overcome us. We can choose to relinquish our joy. Why else would David pray, "Restore to me the joy of your salvation" (Ps. 51:12) if it wasn't something he had lost?

The Holy Spirit is the One who instills joy in us, but He can use us as instruments to bring it about in others through encouragement. When we speak words of upbuilding, we involuntarily raise people's spirits. This is not something we may even be consciously trying to do. It just happens.

I might be feeling rotten when I awaken on Sunday morning, but I force myself to go to church. I still feel lousy as I walk in the door, wishing I had stayed home. Before I can make it to my seat, I receive a few hellos, a couple of hugs, an "I love you"—and I'm on top of it before I even sit down. After the service there is more of the same. As I let people touch me, their spontaneous love fills my heart with the joy of being a part of the body of Christ.

We need each other's encouragement to restore the joy of our salvation.

ENCOURAGEMENT . . . REVIVES THE SOUL

Picture, if you can, your soul lying unconscious on the ground. Encouragement happens along and administers mouth to mouth resuscitation. If you can conjure up this ridiculous image, you'll have an idea of how essential encouragement is to the health of our souls.

Have you ever wanted to quit? Have you ever been infected with the I've-had-it syndrome and planted your feet in cement, vowing never to move again? Then, just in the nick of time, right before the concrete hardens, someone drops this on you: "I'm so glad you're in my life. I thank God for you. Let me take this opportunity to tell you why. . . ."

Time stops momentarily. The concrete erodes. You're released and plod on.

If that person had not touched your life, someone else might have. But then again, probably not. You would have embedded yourself in the cement of defeat, failure, and bitterness. Once such an attitude takes hold it's next to impossible to crack.

Encouragement takes on a new sense of urgency when we reflect on those dear members of the body of Christ whom we are losing every day for lack of such support. The once-active and productive areas in the lives of these members wither and die because we fail to build them up. We prevent them from attaining abundant life by figuratively stepping on their spiritual oxygen lines. But when we do succeed in our endeavors to revive the soul of a discouraged brother or sister, newfound abilities and the confidence to perform as God intended are released within that individual.

ENCOURAGEMENT . . . RELEASES CONFIDENCE

It takes only one person who believes I can accomplish a goal to make me want to try. I have one friend who has continued to assure me throughout our relationship that she believes in me. Possibly others have a measure of faith in me, too, but Sharon is the one who repeats it aloud periodically. And I need to hear that because I don't always believe in myself. Actually, very seldom do I believe in myself. Yet, I rest assured in the glow of Sharon's faith in me because it never falters. It is the spark I need: "If Sharon believes I can, maybe I can. If Sharon believes I am capable, maybe I am."

So I try my wings, and oftentimes I can fly. Oh, sure, I crash once in a while, but it's not because Sharon doesn't believe in me. It's because I look down and get scared. There I lie, a crumpled mass of bruised humanity and faithful Sharon is patching up the holes, all the while reminding me, "I believe in you, you know. You can. . . . You are. . . ."

We release confidence in one another in a variety of ways: (1) by knowing what the Word says about who we are and what we can do and then affirming others with the Scripture; (2) by noticing godly qualities in others and acknowledging them aloud; (3) by standing beside self-doubters and refusing to leave until they try; (4) by believing in them for what they can't see, based on our faith in them; (5) by nurturing a "try, try again" attitude when things don't go well.

You may be someone's last hope. If you don't believe in that person, who will?

ENCOURAGEMENT . . . RELIEVES PRESSURE

The pressure to perform, to succeed, to be perfect eats away at all of us. Constant attempts to live up to the expectations of others can cause extreme stress, leaving us with the ever-present feeling of being perched precariously atop a cliff, ready to throw ourselves down at the first symptom of failure.

Believe it or not, we can release that pressure in one another through encouragement. At a time when I felt like a loser, a failure, a complete washout, Iris unknowingly did just that for me.

"You're a godly woman," she began. "You're going through a difficult time right now and you're not spewing all over everyone. You're the epitome of a godly woman in our midst. . . ." As she went on, I began to blubber all over her, which totally threw her. Iris thought she must have hurt me and couldn't understand what had brought on the tears.

I had been feeling like a nothing, yet someone whom I esteemed highly still considered me a godly woman. The momentary emotion of this thought was more than I could handle, but what a refreshing release!

Here are a few ways you can encourage others by relieving pressure.

"No one loves me," says a troubled teenager.

"I love you," you reply.

Pressure released.

"I can't do anything right," a co-worker comments.

"I've watched the way you treat your wife. You're a good husband," you say.

Pressure released.

"Why did that family leave the church?" from a discouraged pastor. "I'm a rotten shepherd."

"Look at the two hundred families who stayed. You're a great pastor," you remind him.

Pressure released.

It's not quite that easy, of course. You may find it necessary to enter into a lengthy dialogue with some who are really down on themselves, but you get the picture.

If your encouragement is used for the purpose of relieving pressure in someone, make sure you're strong enough to withstand the force of the pressure being released. It may explode with vehement emotion. Don't take it personally. Anyway, you asked for it when you committed yourself to become an encourager.

ENCOURAGEMENT . . . REPELS NEGATIVE THINKING

When I start thinking negatively, I usually carry it through to where I start acting on my thoughts. Somewhere down the road a friend ends up helping me pick up the pieces of my life, shattered because of my actions during this period. I disgust myself sometimes, but I'm grateful that another's encouragement has intercepted the self-destructive process of negative thinking and set me back on the path to recovery.

I am not suggesting that we begin to counter everyone's negative statements with a positive rebuttal. Super-positive Pollyanna can be a pain in the neck, if you know what I mean, especially when one is down.

"Like one who takes away a garment on a cold day, or like vinegar poured on soda, is one who sings songs to a heavy heart" (Prov. 25:20). Save your songs—pleeease. There is a delicate balance between singing songs to a heavy heart and encouraging one caught in the negative thinking trap.

Here's what not to do:

"I'm feeling really rotten today. What a lousy day."

"Oh, but this is the day that the Lord has made. Rejoice and be glad in it."

"How can I rejoice when my husband walked out on me last night, my son just announced he wants to marry a belly dancer I've never met, and my doctor just informed me I have a bleeding ulcer? And now the garbage disposal is plugged up."

"Count your blessings. You have a roof over your head."

"It leaks."

"You have healthy kids. And belly dancing is good exercise. Maybe she could teach you. . . ."

"Oh, shut up."

Likewise you don't want to be someone who clucks his or her tongue in sympathy, saying, "Poor you. Life is rotten all right. Let's drop out."

But here is what you can do:

"I'm sorry you're having a rotten day. What's the problem?"

Grumble, complain, gripe, growl.

"That's rough, all right. How can I help?"

Shrug.

"Let's take a look at your options."

"Options? What are you talking about?"

"You're strong. This won't destroy you. You can choose how you're going to respond to this lousy day."

"I can? I don't have to commit suicide?"

"I won't let you. You're an important part of my life. I love you."

"You do? Wow!"

Encouragement never laughs in the face of hopelessness. It never pooh-poohs misery by putting on a big smile and saying, "Think positive. It's mind over matter."

Instead, encouragement supports, affirms, and prods with words like, "C'mon, you can make it!" It never judges, never condemns, never ridicules. As darkness flees in the brilliant presence of light, so negative thinking fades in the bold assertion of encouragement.

ENCOURAGEMENT . . . REDEEMS
EMOTIONAL DAMAGE

In the aftermath of an emotional vortex, encouragement helps someone pick up the pieces and fit them back together. It heals, soothes, redeems, and uplifts the faltering human spirit.

Any trial or testing drains one's energy for living. My emotions can take a beating even performing the simple task of putting my five children to bed at night. What should be a loving and fairly easy undertaking can become a major trauma in a matter of minutes.

Sometimes it seems that the telephone is nothing less than the last vulturous deterrent to my final peace of mind at the end of a long day. Inevitably in rings just as I sink down into my easy chair after hearing the last prayer from number five. Yes, I will admit that when I hear certain voices on the other end, I'm tempted to offer my regrets to the caller about Gloria's unexpected demise and for further information, refer them to the next of kin.

In contrast, when certain other voices greet me from the other end of the line, my heart leaps with excitement as I settle down for a meaningful conversation with a dear friend. I marvel that my heart can still leap when I'm so exhausted. I can only attribute it to the fact that I know I'm going to receive an earful of positive reinforcement and encouragement and that I'm going to come away from the dialogue refreshed and strengthened.

Encouragement diligently sews up the ragged and torn edges of our emotions caused by nervousness, exhaustion, and heartache.

You may look at someone who is suffering emotional damage and wonder if your efforts are really worth the time and trouble. No doubt about it, encouragement is a lot of work, probably some of the hardest work you'll ever do. And you won't always immediately see the rewards of your labor, if you ever see them at all.

A few indicative signs in the objects of your encouragement make it worthwhile: (1) dull eyes that begin to sparkle again, (2) once-slumped shoulders thrown back in unwavering confidence, (3) a newfound desire to serve God rather than go under, (4) renewed hope where lack of purpose once prevailed.

ENCOURAGEMENT . . . RENEWS HOPE

Hope is an ambiguous word that escapes precise definition much of the time. It's the feeling that what we desire, what we are praying for, will someday materialize.

How does encouragement renew hope? It reminds one of the good things that are lying ahead, when all that can be seen with the naked eye is heartache and more trouble.

The hopeless are characterized by such hyperboles as:

"This *always* happens to me."

"My life will *never* be better."

"Nothing good *ever* happens to me."

"This is absolutely the *worst* time of my entire life."

Encouragement doesn't immediately jump in with: "Things could be worse. You could be living on the streets of Calcutta [or married to my wife, or confined to a wheelchair, or . . .]." Since no one can ever completely comprehend another's pain, who can say what's "worse" than something else?

What encouragement does do is remind the hopeless of (1) their position in Christ, (2) past triumphs over failure, (3) what to be thankful for in the present, (4) what to look forward to in the future.

". . . Christ in you, the *hope* of glory" (Col. 1:27). Whatever tragic loss the hopeless suffer, their relationship with the Lord remains intact. As believers, we always have reason for hope and can encourage each other with that.

Why bother to encourage one another? That's the question we set out to answer at the beginning of this chapter.

The Gift of Encouragement

Does encouragement have a purpose? Is it worth the effort? What do *you* think?

TIME TO CONSIDER

1. Why encourage? List five reasons why God wants his people to encourage each other.

2. How do you resist the urge to offer quick platitudes when someone is hurting? What do you do instead?

3. How do you recognize a hopeless person? What can you do to encourage the hopeless and restore hope?

4. A negative thinker is set on a course. How can your encouragement reverse the negative thinker's direction?

5. Some people are walking pressure cookers. How can your encouragement help them release steam? When the steam spews your direction, how do you handle it?

4

...

Some How-To's of Encouragement

I find it remarkable that the act of encouraging others is not innate in the character of the Christian. Does it not seem only reasonable that at the point of becoming born again we should automatically begin living solely for others rather than ourselves and constantly striving for ways and means of building them up?

Unfortunately, it's not that simple. True, many naturally altruistic people seem to just ooze with sincere words of praise and commendation for others. They never say a negative word about anyone, never gossip, and just generally seem to be nice folks. On the other hand, there are people like me who have to work really hard at being nice. I don't think there's a kind bone in my body. Those wonderful fruits of the Holy Spirit mentioned in Galatians 5:22, 23 do not come readily to me. I grunt and groan and pray a lot.

The Gift of Encouragement

Paul instructed the Colossians to ". . . clothe yourselves with compassion, kindness, humility, gentleness and patience" (Col. 3:12). Whereas some people slip into these clothes easily, as if they were tailor-made, I have to push and pull and stretch and jerk to get even an arm or a leg in. If I do manage to get on the whole garment, it is usually pulling apart at the seams or unraveling altogether by the end of the day.

However, to look on the bright side, since I lean (or is it catapult?) toward being critical, when I *do* encourage or praise you, it's because I really mean it from way down deep in my gut.

As you can plainly see, encouragement is definitely not inherent in my nature. I had to be taught how to do it.

I hesitate here to go any further, lest you misinterpret the following guidelines as a step-by-step formula for encouragement. I refuse to reduce encouragement to a formula. If there is such a thing, it is enclosed in the four-letter word CARE, which we discussed in a previous chapter. If you feel you have moved past that point, you can implement the ensuing suggestions as simply a means to an end, for performing any one of them alone will not make you an encourager. Encouragement is a work of the Holy Spirit in the human heart, causing us to truly care—to desire the very best for one another.

With that in mind, may I suggest some very practical methods to help you become a lifestyle encourager?

BE SPECIFIC

Paul is a prominent example of an encourager. Read any of the Epistles and you will find specific words of encouragement. He told the Philippians it was good of them to share in his troubles (Phil. 4:14). To the Colossians he wrote that he had heard of their faith in Christ Jesus and their love for all the saints (Col. 1:3, 4). In his letter to the Romans he thanked God for them because their faith was being reported all over the world (Rom. 1:8).

We Christians are guilty of using, abusing, and misusing the word *bless*.

"You sure blessed me last week when we were together."

"I did? How's that?"

"Oh, just everything you said was so good."

That sure doesn't tell me a lot. I can barely remember my name some days, let alone what I said last week.

Don't get me wrong. I'll gladly accept any compliment and tuck it away. The fact that I blessed someone and was actually told so . . . well, that person is to be commended. But if it was me in the preceding conversation I wouldn't have let that individual get away with telling me I blessed her or him. The discussion would have continued thus:

"What did I say that blessed you?"

"Oh, something about my being a good mother."

"Refresh my memory. I know you're a good mother, but what did I say that blessed you?"

"You said you thought I was sensitive or something." Hem. Haw. Blush.

"Oh, you're talking about when Johnny came into the room pouting and how you gently brought the problem to the surface? It's true. You really are sensitive."

"My husband thinks I'm too harsh with the kids, and I'm always working and praying about being more gentle."

Ah—finally. Now I know why it blessed her. She needed to hear those particular words because of her struggle in that area. Now that I know that, I will watch more carefully and encourage her again when I see growth in her sensitivity.

"I am so blessed."

What in the world does that mean? It could mean anything from excitement over the new pair of shoes you bought today to relief at finally marrying off your youngest child.

For the novice encourager, here are some initial phrases to help get you started in being specific. The seasoned encourager uses them without even thinking about it.

"I love you because. . . ."

"I see in you. . . ."

"You're so good at. . . ."

"I really like the way you. . . ."

"You always make me feel. . . ."

BE HONEST, YET KIND

Many times only a fine line exists between encouragement and flattery or manipulation; we'll deal with this in more detail in a later chapter. But being honest means that we will encourage others only when we can do so with veracity. We don't want to become known as flatterers.

Perhaps you're thinking, *Wouldn't it be better to be dishonest so as not to hurt someone's feelings?* No—there are ways to work around this dilemma. Take for instance the proud mother who shoves her new baby boy under your nose and eagerly awaits your admiring response. Since he's the homeliest infant you've ever seen, you're temporarily immobilized while you search frantically for the right words. Here are some possibilities:

"Oh, what a beautiful head of hair," or if he's not only homely but bald, "What tiny fingers. Aren't babies precious?" or simply "What a sweet baby."

The mother's feelings are spared, and you have maintained your stance of encouragement.

Paradoxically, being honest may at times mean not

encouraging—it may mean keeping silent. However, when you're known as an encourager, people look to you for input. They know you're thinking something, so when you're quiet, they naturally assume your thoughts are negative. Otherwise you would probably verbalize them. To avoid these awkward occasions, I've learned to look for some positive factor in every situation and every person with whom I connect. When I find it, I speak out.

BE ASSERTIVE

One dictionary definition of the word *assertive* implies being positive or confident in a persistent way. If we're not assertive, others won't take us seriously when we encourage them.

I have a friend who periodically will sit me down, look me right in the eyes, take my hand, and boldly state, "I see so much growth in you in the area of . . ." or "You mean so much to me because. . . ." I won't bore you with the details, but you get the picture. Sometimes she sends a note telling me how wonderful I am and why.

How can I not believe her? She's so sure she knows what she's talking about. I may not feel wonderful, but I choose not to argue the point with someone who is so unyielding in her confidence in me.

Such motions as shifting the eyes and shuffling the feet can negate our encouragement. But when I look into your eyes, I'm saying, "Hey! Listen! Because you're so important, what I'm about to say is important!" When I take your hand, I'm saying ". . . and the reason I'm telling you this is because I care so much about you." The self-assured inflection in my voice means, "I've thought this through, and I know that what I'm speaking is true. Therefore you can believe me."

Be a bulldog, not a bulldozer. Hang on tenaciously to

your confidence, but don't get pushy about it.

BE SPONTANEOUS

There are definitely times when we need to think through our words, but encouragement can lose its spontaneity, its freshness, its sincerity if it's overrehearsed.

If I would listen to my heart instead of my head, I'd be okay. But my head speaks so much louder than my heart that it tends to drown out my feelings altogether.

I remember wanting to encourage Debbie, a friend who had led our monthly women's meeting for the first time and done a fine job. Everything had flowed smoothly, and she deserve to be told so. Immediately after the meeting a lot of women gathered around Debbie, and I assumed they were all complimenting her on her leadership ability. I mingled with the other women while my head and heart were arguing:

"She doesn't need me to tell her when so many others already have."

"You're not 'so many others.' She needs to hear it from you."

"That's silly. Who am I? Just one more star in the sky, grain of sand on the beach, tree in the forest . . . [ad nauseam]."

"She cares about what you think."

"I doubt it."

At this point I found myself face to face with Debbie. Everyone else had drifted away.

"Debbie, you did a great job of leading the meeting tonight," I blurted out. "It ran so smoothly. You seemed so relaxed. You really have a way of making people feel comfortable."

She grabbed my hand. "Honest? I did okay? You don't know how I needed to hear that. Nobody else has said anything, and I was feeling that maybe I'd bombed."

Enough said about listening to one's heart instead of one's head.

When I'm teaching Bible study, sometimes I use one of the women in the group as a positive example for a point I'm trying to make. I spontaneously praise her in front of everyone, and her sense of self-worth begins to soar. Words of encouragement take on new significance when shared in front of others.

DON'T WORRY ABOUT THE RECEPTION

Reception should be the least of our worries. Doesn't everyone love to be praised? You would think so. However, some people are so insecure that they go into shock when they hear anything good about themselves. They will even stand and argue with you.

"Who, me?" Mouth and eyes widen in surprise. "You must be thinking of someone else."

"No, I'm talking about you."

A violent shake of the head. "It can't be. Really? Me? No. . . ."

By this time you're beginning to wonder if it's worth the effort. It is, though. The insecure ones need to hear it more than anyone else.

When you compliment someone you may receive this response, "Oh, it's not me. It's the Lord." Or, "You must need glasses." You may even reach out to hug someone and find yourself up against an unyielding board of rigidity.

These three examples comprise maybe 5 percent of the responses received from encouraging others, but I mention them because they do happen. Probably 95 percent of the time the other person will beam all over the place when encouraged.

The point is, "Do not withhold good from those who

deserve it, when it is in your power to act" (Prov. 3:27).

How your encouragement is received cannot be allowed to undermine your obedience to God in relaying the message. If you dwell too much on how your actions will be received you'll never get around to doing them because you will visualize some ridiculous scenario in which you'll end up looking like a fool.

BE CONSISTENT

Are you a person who can be depended upon for encouragement? Do others look to you for input because they know you and are confident that you always see the best in them? It's not that you are blind to the whole picture. Certainly our weaknesses are on public display much of the time, despite our careful diligence in attempting to hide them. But you can choose to minimize my weaknesses and maximize my strengths, thereby making me a better person—we all respond much more positively to encouragement than we do to criticism.

Once in the habit of building up others, you won't be able to be with people anymore without doing it.

If you are not yet to the place where this seems natural for you, set a goal of: (1) not leaving church, Bible study, work, school or any other group until you have encouraged at least one person, (2) speaking at least one encouraging statement anytime you are one-on-one with your family or friends, (3) sending at least one or two notes of encouragement a month.

Soon these guidelines will not even enter your consciousness because such actions will become by-products of your inner nature as encourager.

BE A TRANSMITTER

Isn't it nice when you discover that people are talking

about you and what they're saying is good? Timeworn gossip, hand-me-down clothes, and used cars may not be so great, but second-hand praise is wonderful indeed. Whenever I'm in conversation with someone who happens to praise a third party, I file away the praise in a mental folder entitled "TO BE TRANSMITTED." Later, when I'm with the third party, I relay the message.

I remember doing this once with the couple who lived across the street from us. They used to engage in some pretty horrible fights right out in front of the entire neighborhood. I mean, they swung with iron pipes. They didn't squabble. They declared war.

One day I asked Kyle if he loved his wife.

"You'd better believe it," he answered gruffly without hesitating. "I couldn't live without the _____."

You could have fooled me, I thought.

The next time I was with Denise, his wife, I told her what Kyle had said.

"Oh really?" She grunted and looked surprised. "I love him too, that ol' _____."

I went back to Kyle and told him that his wife really loved him. They must have never told each other because this was obviously news to him.

"She told you that?" he asked incredulously. "That she loves me?"

Kyle and Denise have since committed their lives to Jesus. I take no credit, but I do believe that the Lord used me to plant some seeds.

This is what's called being a transmitter—bearing words of encouragement from one person to another person.

How often do we commend those who aren't present to those who are? Our words of appreciation can spill out into infinity, yet never fall on the ears of those who need to hear them the most.

The Gift of Encouragement

It gives me great joy to see how my words of transmission bless another person. Maybe you've only thought of "transmission" as an auto part. If so, you're not too far off because a car's transmission relays motive force from the engine to the wheels. As I transmit words from one person's heart (engine) to another, it can propel that second person to action. For encouragement always makes us want to reach higher, to move forward into all God has for us.

BE THERE

The simple act of showing your face can be an encouragement in itself. Just being there sometimes speaks louder than anything else you could do or say.

I must admit I'm not one for being anywhere unless there's an awfully good reason. I love people, but detest meaningless social occasions. Figure that one out if you can. (I've tried.)

I do not attend weddings, showers, or Tupperware parties simply because I am invited. I sit down and thoroughly analyze the situation from all angles. Will it really make a difference to anyone if I'm there? Will anyone even know whether I'm there? Will anyone care? Granted, I may carry this to an extreme at times, but I hate to waste precious hours small-talking at meaningless social functions. Even more than that, I hate the uncomfortable feeling I usually get around people I don't know.

But if my presence somewhere will be an *encouragement* to even one person, I'll be there quicker than you can even speak the word. "Being there" may be inconvenient at times. It may conflict with your schedule or goals. It may mean putting your life "on hold"—for right now, anyway.

Some people swoop down into our lives and are gone as quickly as they came. Some come in, their mouths flapping and never shut up the whole time. Others appear and disappear at such regular intervals that you get their fronts mixed up with their backs. Some sneak in with a pea-shooter, always looking for an opening, and some come with a plunger, completely sucking all life out of you before they leave.

A few are *there* for you. They may not say much; they may not do much. But you feel the warmth of their presence, you hear their whispered prayers, you see the traces of tears for you on their cheeks.

They are there. Not next door. Not down the street. But there, with you, alongside you—showing they care by being close.

Let's be there for one another.

How we encourage others depends on the person and the situation. No method will work 100 percent of the time for each person. If it did, we would not need the Holy Spirit. So, in the final analysis, it is not a matter of eeny-meeny-miney-moe as to which method to use. Instead, it's "Holy Spirit, I see a need. How do you want me to respond?"

TIME TO CONSIDER

1. How can you be more assertive in encouraging others? What would give you more confidence?

2. Is there anyone in your life now for whom your presence is making a difference? How are you "there" for others?

3. Have you ever withheld "good from those who deserve it when it is in your power to act" (Prov. 3:27)? Why? How can you deal with negative feelings that cause you to withhold encouragement when you know others need it?

The Gift of Encouragement

4. Can others depend on you for encouragement? Why or why not?

5. How can you be more spontaneous in encouraging others? How can you worry less about another's response and be free to deliver an encouraging word no matter what?

5
...
When and Where to Encourage

Timing is a significant factor in building up others. In this chapter, we'll look at how certain times and places are more conducive to encouragement than others.

Immediately after your daughter trips over her feet and falls on her face is not the time to tell her how graceful she is. She may indeed be a rather graceful individual, but her agility was hardly in evidence at that point. Tell her another time. What could be an encouragement in this case is your concern over whether or not she hurt herself. Or, if her face is the color of a ripe tomato as she scrambles to her feet, you might be able to assure her that no one else saw her fall.

Because we have this need to appear always poised and "together" in public, when we exhibit any less than a perfect image, our self-esteem suffers a terrible blow. One does need encouragement at such times. But remember in whatever you say or do that timing is an important element in the act of encouraging.

A friend who knew little about the basic concepts of encouraging asked me *when* she should do it: "Twice a week, monthly, whenever I feel like it?"

I'm afraid she may have missed an important point. Again, there is no strict formula. You can't go to bed at night and lie there wondering if you administered your proper ration of encouragement that day. If you think you haven't, there is no sense in nudging your sleeping spouse and saying, "You cooked my bacon and eggs just right this morning." It just doesn't work that way.

However, the Bible makes it clear when to encourage: "But encourage one another daily, as long as it is called Today . . ." (Heb. 3:13).

That can be twenty times day or just once. But "daily" means *every day.* If we are to do this every day, we must remain alert to those times when the Lord brings others across our paths, whether they come to us or whether we venture out to meet them. Now let's look at some of the places where these encounters can happen.

AT HOME

The biggest challenge to you in your role as encourager may very well be your own home. It's analogous to learning to drive with a stick shift. If you can master a stick, you can drive almost any vehicle. (I said "almost." I drove a tractor for the first time recently, and it wasn't quite the same as cruising around town in my Pinto.) If you can encourage your family to whose faults you're exposed on a daily basis, you can encourage almost anyone.

Because home is a haven away from the high-performance expectations of the outside world, we tend to relax a little too much. We get too comfortable and slide into the Hey-don't-bug-me syndrome whereby we feel that we should be catered to, no matter how we act or what we say. We arrogate to ourselves the right to act like a creep if that's how we feel—because, after all, we're "at home."

Why is encouragement within the family structure so imperative? One reason is that for most of us a large portion of each day is consumed with work or school during which time we are often victims of others' subjective criticism. If we can depend on our families to build us up, it will mitigate the criticism.

Occasionally during family devotions I will ask each member of the family to make a positive statement about all of the other members. It goes something like this:

"Grant, what do you like about Travis? What makes him so special to you?"

"He lets me sleep in his bedroom sometimes." Or . . . "He eats my vegetables when no one's looking."

Sometimes the whole exchange gets a little gushy: "Mom, what I like about you is that you always listen to me. You're one of my best friends. I can talk to you and know you really care."

I hurry them off to bed then, before I blubber all over everyone. They may have been bickering with each other most of the day, but after hearing all of this strong, positive input, they usually go to bed hugging and laughing.

Praise is not always so easily facilitated. Someone may have had a bad day or, for no apparent reason, chooses to be a grump. We save that person until last, and—after that individual hears how wonderful he or she is and sees that there is still acceptance even in such a grouchy state—participation can often be somewhat hesitantly initiated.

Home—a place you can let down your defenses and expose your weaknesses, knowing you'll be rebuilt.

57

AT CHURCH

Too often we rush in and out of church without really *seeing* the people around us. Some of my most satisfying encounters have occurred during those few moments before and after the service. When I'm feeling low, I tend to want to stay away from church because I don't want to face people. If I give in to this impulse, I usually sink lower. But if I force myself to go to church, not only for the worship and teaching, but for the body of Christ—His people—I will, more often than not, come away feeling shored up. In other words, we must make ourselves available for encouragement to take place. I remember a particular service where the worship leader asked anyone who felt so inclined to stand and verbally encourage another person in the congregation. Everyone was on the edge of his or her seat, eagerly waiting a turn to express some deep, heartfelt feeling for someone else.

"Therefore, as we have opportunity, let us do good to all people, especially to those who belong to the family of believers" (Gal. 6:10). Our uppermost responsibility as encouragers is to our brothers and sisters in the body of Christ. The church is a stabilizing force in the world today. If we're not encouraging one another, we have nothing in our reserve tanks with which to minister to a hopeless world.

It troubles me deeply when, instead of encouraging, I see the church pointing a finger, condemning, preaching, superciliously judging—taking on what she feels is her primary God-given mission, to come down on everyone's sin.

Granted, sin cannot be justified. I hate the sin that still resides in me. I would give anything to be perfect, but because I have not yet attained a glorified body, I still sin. I know most of my own weaknesses, so I don't need constantly to be reminded of them. What I need is for someone to tell me what to do about them—to give me hope.

Please, before I lie down and quit because of all the work that still needs to be done in me—can you tell me one thing I'm doing right? If I can't depend on my spiritual family to encourage me, who *can* I depend on?

AT WORK OR SCHOOL

Because we are so closely connected to many of those with whom we work or go to school, we can too easily take them for granted and completely overlook their needs.

How much job burnout could be prevented if we were to begin to encourage those in high-pressure positions? How many students who consider themselves losers would persist in that line of thinking if they had even one person in their lives whom they could count on to build them up on a daily basis?

Tomorrow, on the way to work or school, instead of focusing on the multiple facets of your daily routine, why not devise a mental list of those in your place of business or study who would benefit from a word of encouragement?

I hold my six-year-old son's teacher in high esteem. My child frequently brings home certificates stating his performance for the day. It may be the Good Listener award or the Good Class Participation award. At any rate, this teacher is quick to praise her students when they've done well, and she is always on the alert for the opportunity to do so.

Since children are constantly under peer pressure to perform—often even severely criticized or ridiculed when that performance falls short of group standards—it's refreshing to know that my son can at least depend on his teacher to notice and commend him on his strengths.

Certain situations at school or on the job lend themselves to negative feedback, especially when working with the public. But by encouraging one another, we can offset these negatives and greatly reduce stress.

AT THE MARKETPLACE

Consider the beauty salon, the grocery store, the post office, and the dry cleaners. Most people approach such establishments with one purpose in mind—to have a specific need met. Time is rarely taken for exchanging niceties, often for no other reason than that there is a long line of customers or appointments strung out in front of the person conducting business.

Encouragement doesn't take long. You don't have to recite a litany of laudable attributes about a person. There's a time and a place for long discourses on what someone means to you, or how much you appreciate the many things he or she has done. The marketplace is probably not the most accommodating place for such tributes, but you can use other ways to spread encouragement there.

To the teller at the bank: "I like to come to your window because you're always so friendly."

To your beautician: "I received so many compliments on my last haircut. You do nice work."

To your car mechanic: "There are so many rip-off artists around. It's great to have a mechanic I can trust."

These businesspeople hear so many gripes and complaints every day that you will be to them as a sparkling shimmer of gold is to a prospector who has hit nothing but dull rock all day. They'll love to see you coming.

When I hired an attorney recently, I anticipated that my case would drag out anywhere from several months to a year. He processed it in a few weeks, thereby saving me much emotional trauma. Because of this professional's efficiency, I was able to start rebuilding my life sooner than if he'd dilly-dallied along. I wrote him a note to let him know how much I appreciated his speed and diligence in settling my case. He did a good job and deserved commendation.

IN GROUPS

One of the most precious acts of encouragement ever bestowed on me took place in a fairly large group of my friends at a party given in my honor. It wasn't my birthday; I wasn't getting married; I wasn't even having a baby (which was unusual since I have one every other year, and this would have been my year). Susie, the hostess, had just decided that I needed to be encouraged. And was she ever on target! She took the initiative in calling a group of my friends together, and they threw me a surprise teddy-bear party. She knows how much I dislike sentimental, mushy stuff, and yet she wanted to do the mushiest thing for me she could think of. What could be more mushy than teddy bears? Thinking I was coming for a potluck supper, I entered the house only to be greeted by a huge heart-shaped banner bearing the words, "We love you, Gloria," and signed by each guest. They sat me down and proceeded to sing me songs they'd written especially for me. They piled all kinds of teddy-bear memorabilia on my lap—stuffed bears in all sizes, posters, a mug, a pin, cards—and with each gift I received a "bear" hug.

They had even baked me a teddy-bear cake.

I cried sweet tears throughout the entire evening because I don't know when I've ever felt more loved.

One reason encouragement is so effective in groups is that in essence each person is saying, "I love you, and I want *everyone* to know why you're so special to me." I've been involved in some groups where they engage in what is called "affirmation times." This works one of two ways. Either each person in turn is the object of everyone's affirmation, or in an unstructured way anyone who feels so inclined may affirm anyone else in the group.

These have been very meaningful times because I have heard others sharing precious gems, treasures from the heart that they might never have expressed had they not been given this unique opportunity.

To hear words of encouragement, even if they are not directed toward you, creates a warm feeling inside. In a group setting, when one person encourages another, *everyone* experiences "warm fuzzies."

This shared and comforting warmth is contagious. A newcomer or a visitor to the group may say to herself: "These people care about each other. Maybe they'll care about me, too." Or someone who's hurting may decide: "If they can accept *her* with all her problems, maybe they'll accept me."

Much ripping and tearing is happening not only in the world, but in the church as well. (It's sad to say, but there is sometimes more in the church.) As members of the body of Christ, we can offer a solid mending for the rips and tears, a place where lives can be rebuilt. Encouragement in groups is one way to provide such a place.

ONE-ON-ONE ENCOUNTERS

By far, most of the encouragement I have both given and received has taken place one-on-one—over the phone, at lunch, driving in the car, before and after group gatherings, anywhere two of us come together for the purpose of sharing a few moments of life.

One-on-one encouragement takes place best when you have another person's undivided attention. Sharing a personal word with someone can be difficult enough without worrying about being interrupted by another someone wanting to chat. For that reason, I find it next to impossible to carry on a meaningful conversation with anyone in a group setting.

Encouragement is not necessarily something to strive for in a one-on-one encounter. It's something that should flow effortlessly from the conversation much as the water flows from the faucet in our sinks. With what seems like so little effort, we receive a vital resource for life.

Many times what we anticipate to be a frivolous lunch with a friend turns out instead to be a lesson in survival as we give or receive those words so desperately needed by one another.

WHEREVER YOU GO

Encouragement needs to happen everywhere. I can think of no exception to this. Once we make the decision to be an encourager, it can happen wherever our feet take us.

It may not always come out right; it may not achieve the desired results 100 percent of the time; people may not believe you—but don't let that keep you from encouraging. For the next place you go, someone may believe you and rise to seemingly insurmountable heights because of your words.

Jesus encouraged people wherever He went. I wonder if He ever felt like saying, "Oh, I quit!" On one occasion when He was preaching to the people, He encouraged them with these words: "I am the light of the world. Whoever follows me will never walk in darkness, but will have the light of life" (John 8:12).

The Pharisees flashed back with: "Oh, sure. Says who? You stand here telling us you're a light. Big deal. Prove it" (free translation).

The Gift of Encouragement

At that point Jesus could have said, "Forget this noise. Who needs it?" Instead He encouraged them even more. Most of them continued to act like knotheads, but at the conclusion of what must have been an exhausting conversation, the Bible says that "even as he spoke, many put their faith in him" (John 8:30).

If we follow our Lord's untiring example and persist in encouragement wherever we go, our efforts will bear fruit.

Where is your next stop? Will it be today, tomorrow, perhaps this weekend?

TIME TO CONSIDER

1. Think of a family member who needs encouragement right now. What would be the most encouraging thing you could do or say?

2. Why are some people more difficult to encourage than others? Is it the way you come across or their inability to receive?

3. What do you think the author of Hebrews meant when he wrote, "Encourage one another daily" (Heb. 3:13)? How can you do that?

4. How can you encourage the people at the businesses you regularly frequent? Your co-workers?

5. Do you encourage non-Christians differently than you do Christians? Why?

6. Jesus encouraged people wherever He went. How can you follow His example?

6
...
Who Needs It?

Who needs encouragement? Everyone—from the President of the United States to the Prince of Wales' valet or the obscure cowhand on a small ranch in Wyoming or the assembly-line worker in a southern textile mill.

How do I know that everyone needs encouragement? After all, the President of the United States has been elected to the most respected governmental position in our country. What does he need to be encouraged about? The fact is, the President shares with you and me one basic similarity: his humanness. Unfortunately, human beings are not indestructible. Without encouragement we can be torn down and destroyed. We can even self-destruct if we choose to. Some of the most influential and powerful people in history have committed suicide. If even one person had lovingly encouraged them, would they have

65

been so quick to take their own lives?

Although we can deduce that everyone needs encouragement, there is no way that time or space will allow us to deal with "everyone." But we can zero in on a few for whom we can identify specific needs.

Dr. Gary Collins, in his book, *How to Be a People Helper,* says this:

Helping relationships differ both in their nature and depth. When two people come together they do not leave their personalities, values, attitudes, insecurities, needs, feelings, perceptions, and abilities at the door. All of these enter into the relationship, and to the extent that people are different, it is likely that no two people ever relate together in a way that is duplicated elsewhere. Consider, for example, how Jesus related to people. He didn't have the same kind of relationship with all of them. With Nicodemus it was intellectual, with the Pharisees it was confrontational, with Mary and Martha it was more relaxed, and with little children it was warm and loving. Jesus recognized individual differences in personality, needs, and level of understanding, and He treated people accordingly. When counselors try to treat all of their counselees in the same way, they fail to build good rapport because they are making the mistake of thinking that all people are alike. All people are *not* alike, and this must be recognized both in the relationships that we build and in the methods that we use.[1]

With that in mind, let's see how to deal with various persons at different emotional levels.

THE FEARFUL

Momentary fear is something that most of us have experienced at one time or another. But worse than that are the icy fingers of dread that wrap themselves around us and entrap us in a prolonged period of anxiety from which we cannot seem to free ourselves.

When we're afraid, our behavior reflects our fear. It's not difficult to spot fearful people. They may shake, cry, bite their nails, laugh too loud, or perform any number of uncharacteristic actions (at least for them) that reveal fear. When I'm afraid, for example, my stomach tightens, my heart palpitates, and I don't say anything—an obvious sign to those who know me that I'm afraid. The more I try to relax, the worse it becomes.

Fear paralyzes. If left undealt with, it can play havoc with our minds, ruin our potential as vessels for God to use, and ultimately destroy our lives. How great it would be if we could detach ourselves from the emotion of fear, step back, look at it objectively, say, "Hmmm, I don't think I need this," and toss it aside.

How I wish it were that simple. Unfortunately, it seldom is. But encouragement can thwart the destruction that fear inevitably produces in our lives. Jesus encouraged the disciples at their points of fear with these words: "Don't be afraid; just believe" (Mark 5:36).

The positive, conscious act of exercising faith will negate fear.

When I first started teaching Bible studies, I was petrified. (I'm not a natural communicator who thrives on speaking to more than one person at a time.) I was so tense that my voice trembled and shook. But, for no other reason than that I believed God to be opening doors that He expected me to walk through, I continued teaching. Fear gradually decreased—and now I love to teach.

"Take courage! It is I. Don't be afraid" (Mark 6:50). We can remind the fearful that Jesus is present and in control of things and that they can commit their scary circumstances to Him and trust Him with the outcome. Jesus dismissed the disciples' fear every time with His words of reassurance. Who or what should we fear in the presence of Jesus Christ?

As David's harp soothed anxious King Saul, so our calm words of encouragement soothe the fearful.

THE ANGRY

It is only in obedience to the Lord that I ever attempt to encourage an angry person. I'm not necessarily referring to the screaming, arm-flailing types, although they would most definitely fall under "the angry category." I'm thinking of those people who walk around with anger raging inside of them and when the right buttons are pushed— boom! an explosion occurs and pity the poor person who pushed the button.

In John Powell's book *Why Am I Afraid to Tell You Who I Am?* he explains:

People who have short fuses and give forth loud noises are frequently reacting to some supposed grievance which is not that which really bothers them. As they cannot discuss openly the real grievance, they are letting off steam and their anger can rarely be taken at face value. What is smoldering in their subconscious is hostility. People are usually far more hostile towards each other than they realize (it is repressed), because our society has conditioned us to believe that hostility is unbecoming in socialized, civilized human beings.[2]

Being such an emotional person myself, I know what I need when I'm angry. Oftentimes what works is for someone to bring me up short, to shock me out of my anger: "Would you stop it! You're acting like a brat."

"Oh, really? I didn't know it showed."

What I don't need is for the people I love to stay away from me, which is exactly what many of them do. Anger is one of the most difficult emotions to confront in others. I am the kind of person who says what she thinks (maybe you've noticed), and when I'm angry, it comes out with a vengeance. That threatens many people and, understandably, they back off to safety.

Anger is a tough one, I will admit. I know of a pastor who attempted to console an angry man who came to his church one day. The confrontation ended with both of them hurtling through a plate-glass window. We must proceed with caution in dealing with angry people.

I've heard nice people (those who rarely get truly angry) make sanctimonious judgments on an angry friend: "Once Fay gets her attitude right, she'll be quite a leader." Or, "If Jim ever gets rid of that chip on his shoulder, we can ask him to be an elder."

When Peter cut off the high priest's ear, Jesus didn't act shocked and say, "Peter, I don't like your attitude. I think you'd better not be an apostle for a while until you get straightened out." What He did do was deal with Peter's anger right on the spot. Since we do not hear anymore about this incident, I assume Peter's status as an apostle did not change one bit.

Even when Peter denied Jesus, he didn't lose his position as an apostle. Jesus didn't even make him prove himself. Peter, after *repenting*—and that is the key word—was forgiven and again immediately restored to good graces. When I am angry, it encourages me when a friend will let

69

me vent my feelings without taking any of my meanness personally. It encourages me to hear, "It's rough all right. I'm so sorry," or to be asked provocative questions so that I can discover my own constructive solution to the cause of my anger. Unfortunately, not many people let me do that. Most of them back off in fear, saying, "I'll see you later when you're feeling better."

An angry person is no threat to me. Actually, it's a challenge to see if I can help the individual. Unless the anger is directed at my personhood (at which time I usually break away), I feel capable of walking others through their anger. Maybe that's because I identify so strongly with that emotion.

In no way am I excusing anger. Uncontrolled anger is sin and must be dealt with. But we can help each other through it. Please don't banish me to my room unless you can come along and sit with me for a while.

Most angry people hate themselves for being angry. Don't write them off. They desperately need your encouragement in the midst of their anger.

THE LONELY

Where anger in a person is many times visible, loneliness is not so easily detected. One reason is that people don't like to admit that they're lonely, so we don't always know who is.

Some people prefer being alone rather than with other people. That need not necessarily mean they are lonely. Others, even when surrounded by human beings, feel alone. Still others are lonely because they have no friends, cannot seem to relate well to others, and do not know how to reach out in friendship. Whatever the cause for loneliness, it is an extremely painful state and can even result in suicide for those unable to cope with it.

How can we encourage the lonely person? The most obvious answer is to be a friend.

I know a woman who seems to relate well to a lot of people in her job as well as at church. She is apparently well liked by many, yet she has confided to me on numerous occasions that she wished she had a friend with whom she could share her innermost thoughts and feelings. I've tried to be that friend, but I don't think I'm the one she needs. Lonely people can be very demanding and often desire more of others than they are capable of giving.

You can encourage lonely people to get involved in various activities. Whether a class, a sport, or a church function, it will fill some time. They will probably still be lonely for a while, but from this exposure to many people, ensuing friendships usually develop. It might be a good idea to take their hand and accompany them to these activities until they feel comfortable on their own.

Lonely people need to know someone is there for them. If you don't have a lot of extra hours, yet feel God has placed a lonely person on your heart, that's okay. Just check in once in a while to show you care. That is what has helped me the most during my lonely times. "I just called because I've been thinking about you so much. How are you?"

The lonely need to know someone is thinking about them, even when not physically in their presence.

THE SORROWFUL

Some people are chronically sad. Have you ever noticed? They go around with a long face all the time. I'm not sure if this is their personality or if they have decided at some point that nothing in life is worth being happy about. Whatever the reason, it's not God's will for anyone to be sad: "be joyful always" (1 Thess. 5:16).

71

Without flaunting your own joy, try to make the sad person laugh. For laughter is a profitable exercise for both spirit and body. "A cheerful heart is good medicine, but a crushed spirit dries up the bones" (Prov. 17:22).

Try to discover the reason why someone seems sad. The source of sorrow may be unknown even to the sad person. It could be an unhappy marriage or an unfulfilling job. Deep-seated sorrow doesn't happen overnight. It can be the result of an accumulation of life's day-to-day pressures, stress that never lets up. If we can encourage the sorrowful to talk through their sorrow, to look for the underlying cause, in the course of discussion they may discover resources for coping that they never knew they had.

You could never convince me that anyone actually likes being sad. If they knew how to change sadness to gladness, they would. In most cases they will cooperate with you when you reach out to help them.

THE GUILT-RIDDEN

You have to catch the guilt-ridden before you can encourage them. They spend a lot of time running from relationships, from people who want to touch and love them. You see, they feel unworthy of your love.

Let me explain the word *guilt-ridden*. First of all being *guilt-ridden* is different from being *guilty*. To be "guilt-ridden" is to be obsessed or dominated by a painful feeling of self-reproach, resulting from a belief that one has done something wrong or immoral. To be "guilty" is to have actual guilt; to deserve blame or punishment. Both the guilty and the guilt-ridden need to be encouraged by the assurance of a generous portion of God's forgiveness. They may also need another's forgiveness—and they certainly need to forgive themselves.

Their actual release from the guilt must come from God

alone. You cannot do that for them. But you can pray for them, and you can be a mouthpiece for the Lord by reassuring them of God's tender mercy, forgiveness, and unconditional love.

Satan uses guilt to paralyze, to lower self-esteem, to render one ineffective for ministry. For when a person is feeling guilty, accompanying the sense of guilt is a feeling of unworthiness and also a preoccupation with self.

The guilt-ridden need to be constantly reaffirmed—reminded that they're not done for. Because of that one area in which they're plagued by guilt, they can easily feel as if their entire life is a waste. They need ongoing support even in the areas where they're still strong because their guilt has blinded them to their strengths.

Dealing with a guilt-ridden person is frustrating. You want to reach out and take the burden of guilt from his or her shoulders, and you cannot. You feel helpless. But dealing with anyone who needs to go through a healing process takes time—yours and mine.

THE JUBILANT

Why do the jubilant need to be encouraged? You may think that if they're so happy, let them do the encouraging. Let's look at some of the reasons why those who wear a smile may need to be encouraged: (1) Jubilance is not a perpetual state of being. It comes and goes like any other emotion. They will not be jubilant forever. (2) Some people are talented actors and actresses. They may appear extremely joyful in public and then go home and cry. They're hurting inside, but they are experts at hiding behind masks. (3) People who seem to have it all together have human needs just like the rest of us. *Everyone* needs encouragement.

It takes a lot to get some people down. My friend Joanne

is like that. Whenever a flaming arrow spins toward her and threatens to pierce her through, she puts on her armor, rises up to deflect the blow and marches ahead toward ultimate triumph, all with a smile on her face. That's not to say that Joanne doesn't cry or experience disappointment or feel like hiding or running at times. Just like you and I, she has those periods of weakness and adversity when she relies on the encouragement of others. Because she's usually such a great encourager herself, other people are forever draining her resources, and she would suffer periodic burnout if she were not built up in return. She's not Superwoman, just a human being who happens to smile a lot.

As for those who wear masks (don't we all at times?), it's not fair to disarm them and rip off their masks. John Powell once again identifies our temptations and admonishes us:

> We are all tempted to unmask others, to smash their defenses, to leave them naked and blinking in the light at the illumination provided by our exposé. It could be tragic in its results. If the psychological pieces come unglued, who will pick them up and put poor Humpty Dumpty Human Being together again? Will you? Can you?[3]

Our objective must be to encourage them to remove their masks themselves by assuring them that we will love them just as much without it. People do not need to wear a perennial smile to gain my affection. As a matter of fact, if they do, I begin to wonder if they are hiding something under their coat.

Don't keep your distance just because a happy person appears to have swallowed a forever-happy pill. You cannot know everything that is going on in that person's heart, and it would behoove you to approach close enough to find out. God may be sending you on a mission of mercy.

THE APATHETIC

"What difference does it make? I don't care." Spoken in anger, those words are not really significant. Spoken in a monotone, however, they indicate that the speaker is in dangerous territory. To be apathetic is to be unmoved, uninterested, unmotivated. If one becomes uninterested in life, he or she may eventually think, *Why not death?*

How can we make anyone care—about anything? Well, we can't *make* them, but we can certainly provide the stimulus to jolt their "caring nerve."

The apathetic person may simply need a change of scenery or a fresh vision. Most often though, apathy sets in when a person doesn't feel that he or she is contributing anything. People who believe they are making no difference in the lives of others may soon stop caring what happens in their own lives. They feel unnecessary, like excess baggage, and may be tempted to heave themselves overboard. When you come across this type of apathy you may be dealing with someone who needs professional help.

I was in an apathetic state once. It's an awful place to be. Nothing moved me. I was finally reached through my identity as a writer. My writing nerve still had a spark of life in it. Small as it was, I realized I could contribute something.

Find that spark in your apathetic friends and build on it. Did they once care about music, church, sports, their children? Stir up that area, prod that nerve. Keep it up until you see someting in them begin to move. If God's kids stop caring, our world has had it. Somehow we must keep caring.

These people and many, many more need our encouragement, for no emotion, positive though it may be, nullifies the human need to be built up. It is a vital part of God's plan and order for His creation.

Look around you. Who do you see needing encouragement?

TIME TO CONSIDER

1. Fear is contagious. What happens inside you when you encounter fearful people? How can you overcome your fear of their fear so that you're free to encourage?

2. An apathetic person can totter dangerously close to the edge of suicide. What can you offer as encouragement to someone who has stopped caring?

3. Have you ever offered platitudes to a grieving person? What encourages someone who is sad? What doesn't?

4. What do you need from God when you're feeling the pangs of loneliness? How can you give that to someone else?

5. How does another's anger affect you? Why is it so difficult to encourage someone who's angry?

7
...

Motivation or Manipulation?

Can something as positive and special as encouragement embrace any dangers? Absolutely. I hesitate to include them because possibly you would never think of them on your own. And in no way do I desire to bring possible tainting to such a pure vehicle which the Lord has given us for building up His people.

At the same time, I would rather warn you of the perils so you'll be alert and ready for them. Otherwise you may stumble up against one, be taken completely off guard, and think, "Yuk! How do I handle this? No one told me this could happen."

I also deem it necessary to predict that others may see flaws in you as an encourager because of the way you facilitate the process, and I want you to be prepared for that, too. Of course, if they don't like the way you encourage, it's their problem—as long as you know you're operating from pure motives.

In his book *Improving Your Serve,* Chuck Swindoll cautions us:

> You will give, forgive, forget, release your own will, obey God to the maximum, and wash dirty feet with an attitude of gentleness and humility. And after all those beautiful things, you will get ripped off occasionally. I want all of us to enter into this ministry of servanthood with our eyes wide open. If we serve others long enough, we will suffer wrong treatment for doing right things. Knowing all this ahead of time will help "improve your serve," believe me.[1]

Satan loves to jam up the works of the kingdom of God, to stop the flow of our ministry to one another, to twist and despoil, painting an evil overtone on anything that God is using for good. I have watched him do this so many times (the Devil is very uncreative and tends to use the same incredibly boring tactics over and over again) that I'm beginning to understand his methods. How tragic it is— but Christians are so blind at times that we play right into his hands.

I've seen him attack encouragers and do it through other brothers and sisters in the body of Christ, the very ones with whom the encourager has expended so much building-up effort. We must be on guard in order, "To keep Satan from getting the advantage over us; for we are not ignorant of his wiles and intentions" (2 Cor. 2:11, AMPLIFIED).

Before you get nervous, think for a minute. Don't pitfalls accompany every good thing we do for God? Missionaries contend with snakes and spiders, and that's the least of their troubles. The closer we draw to God and the more we serve Him, the more of a threat we become to the kingdom of darkness. Satan will do his best to discourage you, to stop your words, to thwart all your efforts to become an encourager. Be mindful of this and encase yourself in the armor of God so you are equipped to resist Satan's attacks.

Enough said about the roaring but toothless lion. Following are some of the specific dangers about which the lifestyle encourager should be aware and forewarned.

MOTIVATION OR MANIPULATION

One day I was explaining to a friend how encouragement can be used to motivate others. She listened carefully and then asked, "Is that motivation or manipulation?" Her question caught me by surprise. It had never occurred to me that encouragement could be used for the purpose of manipulation. But as I thought about it, I had to admit that encouragement *could be* used as a form of manipulation. Although we may never knowingly encourage someone for self-serving reasons, we should recognize that when encouragement is used for that purpose, it becomes deceitful, evil, and sinful. Let's look at some examples of encouragement used as manipulation.

Let's say you ask your daughter to bake a batch of cookies because you need them that night for some unexpected company. You know she's inclined to not only move, but move faster on praise, so when you casually mention that she makes the best chocolate chip cookies you've ever tasted, you're using encouragement to manipulate.

Or perhaps you are the chairman of the church bazaar and need another worker. You phone Dorothy and she sounds reluctant. "Oh, I don't know if I want to help this year," she answers your plea in a tired voice.

You panic. You are depending on her. "Oh, but Dorothy, you're the most faithful and dependable worker I have. I especially wanted to have you at the ticket table because you're so friendly and always make everyone feel welcome. It won't be the same without you."

"Really? I'm that important? Well, I suppose one more year won't hurt."

Mission accomplished. Unsuspecting Dorothy has been manipulated. She has agreed to what you wanted, which is perhaps not in her own best interest. Anytime you encourage someone for the purpose of accomplishing or furthering your own goals—with little regard for what is right for them—you're manipulating. And when that person catches on, you will be despised and resented for your tactics and possibly not trusted again.

If you're insecure and encourage others because you want to be liked and thought of as a wonderful person, you're manipulating for the purpose of enhancing your own reputation.

I'm not advocating that you sit down and analyze each and every impulse of encouragement until your enthusiasm has been destroyed. Just be careful that your reason for building up the other person is for them—not for you.

BEWARE OF THE SUPERPERSON IMAGE

The more you become known as an encourager, the more people will get the impression that you're this great wonder, forever on a divine high, a tower of strength and never in need yourself.

Encouragers sometimes intimidate others because of their consistent reaching out and inevitable confidence in doing so (the more you do it, the more adept you will become). Their Superperson image makes other people feel inadequate. The encourager needs encouragement. So when those known for their strength suddenly become weak, they often stand alone. They cannot turn to those who have depended on them for encouragement, for at the first sign of weakness in a fearless leader, immaturity may cause the followers to seek out another leader—one who is strong for them. The encourager can look to other known encouragers, but they are often so busy encouraging their weakers brothers and sisters that they don't have time for their peers. Most often, the lifestyle encourager's needs are met directly by the Lord.

However, if you let it be known at the onset of your association that you, too, are sometimes in need of encouragement, you may be able to avoid the heavy responsibility of being known as Superperson.

As an effective encourager, you most likely want to share your own weaknesses and trials anyway, so others will know that your concern arises not from piety, but from your own times of pain and suffering and doubts. This can engender in the encourager a healthy ability to sense when others are hurting and in need of a supportive hand.

I must admit that I tend to place people on pedestals. Once I begin to care deeply for a person, I cannot be convinced that he or she is any less than totally wonderful and close to perfect, no matter how many shortcomings they admit. You will not always be successful in knocking your own pedestal out from under you. People will manage to keep it intact or erect a new one if it is damaged. But keep trying. If they're around you long enough, their eyes will be opened. Better yet, ask them if you can move in for a while. That will do it.

DON'T ALLOW YOURSELF TO BE TAKEN ADVANTAGE OF

Certain individuals, if you express the slightest bit of interest in them, will drain you for all you're worth. Encouragers, because of their availability and willingness to give of themselves, can easily be walked upon. No person has the right to take so much from you that you have nothing left to give anyone else or even yourself.

Beware of those who call constantly, who hang on you at church, who make unrealistic demands on your time. Encouragers spread themselves thin as it is, and if one person is consistently draining them, it's not fair to all the others who depend on them for support.

Don't feel that it is up to you to meet every need that presents itself. God has many soldiers in His army, and He has equipped them with the spiritual tools they need for their individual missions. Although the role of encourager is to be played by every soldier in the army, some are better equipped than others for certain situations and specific kinds of folks.

If you find yourself in a friendship where the other person seems to be depending on you too often and for more than you feel able to give, step back and ask the Lord exactly what it is you are to provide for that person. It may be far less than what is currently being required of you. Learn to say no and don't feel guilty in doing so. Some people's chief need is to grow up, and you can help them do so by backing off and letting them steer their own ship.

Please don't take this wrong. I'm not suggesting that you pray thirty minutes every time before encouraging others. Some people pray long prayers about everything from what color socks to wear in the morning to what brand of toothpaste to buy. (Grocery shopping must take them forever.) Use discretion here, but be aware that certain people send us to our knees—whether out of a need to look to the Lord or out of sheer exhaustion at the demands placed on us.

DON'T BECOME MAUDLIN

When you encourage others, choose strong words to express your heart and let them stand on their own. There's no need to sugar-coat them with a drippy, sticky syrup.

You can say, "You're so sweet," to someone in a strong tone of voice chock-full of true feeling that comes from deep within. *Or* you can say, "You're so sweet," in a goochie-goochie-goo tone of voice that makes one sick to one's stomach.

I like to believe that Christians do not ridicule or scorn others, at least outwardly, but behind the scenes a maudlin person may be laughed at. Those overly sentimental women in the movies always are. Even when people do not laugh out loud, they may be snickering to themselves, "Cut the slop!" They might even add, "What do you want?" when you are only trying to encourage them.

Perhaps you have been operating on the principle that "if a little is good, a lot will be better. Do it all the way. Pour it on thick." *Not so.* This is not Broadway and we're not characters in a theatrical production speaking Shakespearean lines in hopes of slaying our audience.

Relax. Sentimentality will kill any positive emotion your words may have stirred in the hearer. If you encourage out of a heart of love, your feelings will be evident without overdramatizing them.

EXPECT NOTHING FROM THE RECEIVER

A trap awaits the encourager who focuses on the responses and reactions of the hearer. This is definitely a temptation once you get a taste of the pleased expression on the face of a person you have just uplifted with your words.

Let's return to Chuck Swindoll's book on servanthood for a moment. He warns:

> If you are the type who needs a lot of strokes from people, who has to be appreciated before you can continue very long, you'd better forget about being a servant. More often than not, you will be overlooked, passed up, behind the scenes, and virtually unknown. Your reward will not come from without, but from within. Not from people, but from the satisfaction God gives you down inside.[2]

Replace the word *servant* with the word *encourager*. It means the same.

It's a heady feeling to know you can affect others' lives in such a positive way—that you can actually motivate others to achieve, to accomplish, to be more than they have ever been before.

The positive response of others is one of the rewards of being an encourager. That's all it is—a reward. It's not an incentive or provocation or the motive for encouraging.

There are two reasons why looking for a positive response is a trap: First, you won't necessarily receive one. And second, instead of focusing on the other person's need, you'll be anticipating the personal satisfaction you'll derive from the encounter.

Don't fall into the habit of predicting what the receiver will do or say. Many people have to think things through before they can respond anyway. Just do it and move on. You have delivered your soul and possibly God's heart to another. What that person does with it is beyond your control. It may be thrown away, it may be held for a while, it may be activated immediately. Whatever is done with it is out of your hands, so let go and release that person from your expectations.

DON'T HIDE BEHIND IT

We can use encouragement as a protective wall behind which we can hide and thereby prevent others from knowing us or reaching out to help us in our need. When others move in too close, we can toss out a bit of encouragement which they (being human) will grab onto. In this way we deter them from coming any closer and even push them back into their own corners. Sorry to say, but just as the skunk throws out his putrid aroma when he feels his territory being invaded, we often throw out encouragement to protect our own interests. Either way, it stinks.

For example, Melissa calls Betty and asks her point-blank how she's doing on her diet. Betty panics. "Oh, okay," she answers casually, fully aware that if the conversation proceeds any further along that line, she will have to reveal that she gained two pounds last week. So Betty redirects the conversation: "I've sure noticed your weight loss, Melissa. You looked so good in that tan suit yesterday. You must be at least a size seven now."

"Oh my, thank you. I have been sticking to my diet for once. As for that new suit, my husband. . . ."

Mission accomplished—Betty's little secret is safe for now.

For another example of hiding behind encouragement, look at Bill and Colleen, a newlywed couple. They are sitting at dinner one evening. Colleen is worried because Bill seems to be distancing himself from her. She decides to approach him about it.

"Bill, is everything okay? You seem so quiet lately.

You're not tired of marriage already, are you?" She twists the napkin in her lap.

Bill, at this point, is not sure how he feels about Colleen and their marriage. He is a little tired of her insistent demands on him when he comes home every night after work. Just once he'd like to be left alone to relax. Instead of using this opportunity to gently share his need with his wife, he uses some words of encouragement to throw her off the track.

"I'm just tired. One thing I do love about marriage is your cooking. It gets better and better. This meat loaf is delicious. It even beats my mom's."

"Oh, Bill, really?"

"Yep."

End of conversation.

Bill is saved from dealing with a very real problem, soon to become a serious issue, and Colleen is temporarily pacified with some phony encouragement which given at any other time would have meant so much more.

Don't use encouragement as a scapegoat. It's too precious to waste while you hide.

AVOID FORMULAS

"Name it and claim it," "positive confession," "seed-faith"—these and other formulas have been mouthed by so many members of the body of Christ and repeated so endlessly that I wouldn't be surprised to hear God yawn. But it's logical—isn't it—to assume that if something works once, it will work again and again and again?

Unfortunately, it's not so simple. As the old saying goes, just as we think we know all the answers, the questions change. This keeps life interesting. It also keeps God on His throne. If we had it all figured out, we wouldn't need God.

Formulas are so comfortable. If you do A, B will follow.

I've known people whom God has healed of cancer. I've also known people who have died of the same disease. Speakers stand before us and spout off formula after formula about faith and physical healing without ever mentioning the possibility that, after all of our fervent praying and pleading with God and our kicking and screaming at Satan (the violent take it by force—another formula), it is still the Lord who is sovereign and He will do as He pleases.

I don't wish to be the one to pop their bubble, but where is this utopia they so simplistically describe as the answer to all of our problems? This beautiful paradise where God is merely a magical genie who shifts into gear as we activate our formulas? This place where I can have anything my heart desires as long as I figure out the spiritual equation?

Elisha instructed the leper Naaman, commander of the army of the King of Aram, to bathe in the River Jordan seven times. Naaman obeyed, and God healed him (2 Kings 5:1–14).

From that point onward, was washing seven times in the Jordan a surefire cure for all lepers? Was it the only cure? What about "Jesus reached out his hand and touched the man. . . . And immediately the leprosy left him" (Luke 5:13)?

Beware of formulas in encouraging. Let God direct you.

DON'T USE ENCOURAGEMENT AS AN EVANGELISTIC TOOL

Some people reach out and encourage for the purpose of converting others. They feed the hungry, give to the poor, and lift up the brokenhearted for one reason: to get them to repent. When they receive no such response, they wipe the dirt off their feet and move on to their next prospect.

Certainly you are to share Jesus with others. Love causes you to move toward others, desiring God's best for them—and Jesus is God's best.

But don't use encouragement to get them to move toward God. That's just another subtle form of manipulation. Watch it!

HANDLING FAILURE

Failure can be a very real stumbling block to you as a lifestyle encourager. "If you're going to do something, do it right or don't do it at all." Let this be our attitude. Kept in check, it provokes us into performing at our highest.

However, we must be realistic. We will sometimes fail in our attempts to encourage others. We may say something stupid. We may move when it's time to stand still. We may rejoice when it's time to mourn. In short, we're going to make mistakes.

Why try? Because a battle is won each time we stumble and rise again. Some warriors suffer through many battles before the war is won. Remember, as an encourager, you're on the winning side. Criticism tears down, but encouragement builds up. Criticism kills the spirit. Encouragement heals the brokenhearted. Criticism defeats. Encouragement equips one for victory.

Here are two principles for handling failure (your own as well as that of others):

1. Decide if it's really a failure. What appears to be failure may not be so in reality. And we know that God can bring good out of the most negative of situations.

2. If, no question about it, you know you've failed, repair what you can and move on. Dwelling on our failures and repeated attempts to patch up our messes can drain us of the energy we need to keep encouraging.

It's okay. Failure will occur less often as you grow in recognizing others' needs and become confident in your ability to meet those needs.

Lest I scare you off forever, I will stop here with the warnings and dangers of building up others. Remember that we rarely trip over these obstacles with our eyes open. Complacency and ignorance are the main culprits. Now that you're aware, stay alert and conscious of the presence of the Lord so you can avoid these entanglements.

TIME TO CONSIDER

1. Have you ever encouraged others for the wrong reasons? How did you get back on track?

2. How can you keep others from taking advantage of you and becoming too dependent on your encouragement?

3. How can you keep from relying on formulas? How can you keep your encouragement genuine?

4. Have you ever thought you were encouraging a person, yet in reality made the person feel worse? If so, how did you recover?

5. Examine yourself to see if your motives for encouraging are pure. Where do you need to improve?

8

...

A Serendipity

The very act of encouraging brings about a great deal of satisfaction. It's pleasing to know that others feel good about themselves because of something you did or said. But you may not be aware of many other built-in rewards accompanying the package of encouragement. These are "extras." They're never something we strive for in encouraging or in any other giving of ourselves to others. They just unexpectedly happen sometimes, and we're pleasantly surprised when they do.

If you're encouraging others for the right reasons—because you genuinely care and want them to bloom and grow in the image of God—nothing blesses you more than to be able to watch their development take place before your very eyes.

Following are a few of the bonuses you will probably

receive in the process of becoming an encourager.

FEEDBACK

"The apostles gathered around Jesus and reported to him all they had done and taught" (Mark 6:30).

Whenever someone encourages me and something positive happens in my life as a result of that encouragement, I try to relay the good news to my encouragers. They need to know they're doing a good job.

Many times people have expressed to me their feelings of appreciation and high esteem for those who have spoken words of encouragement that have resulted in significant life changes.

"Well, have you told him what's happened?" I ask.

A look of surprise. "No, I guess I should do that."

"Of course you should do it—immediately!"

If you make the decision to become an encourager (and it is a decision that merits considerable thought on your part before you embark on such a giant undertaking), the odds are you'll receive feedback at various points on this venture.

I spoke on "encouragement" to a women's group recently, and as is naturally the case, the listeners were encouraged in the process. I have never seen such a responsive group as this bunch. I would not exaggerate if I said that afterwards at least three-fourths of the entire group, in turn, grabbed me, hugged me, and expressed their total appreciation in my coming and sharing a teaching they desperately needed. I couldn't get out the door for at least an hour after I finished speaking. It wasn't any one thing I said or my magnetic charm that moved them. These women needed to be encouraged, and that is what they responded to. I, in turn, was built up by their positive response.

I know of a lady who asks for written feedback after every Bible study she teaches and after every speaking engagement, whether it's a retreat or a seminar. In doing this, she is teaching lifestyle encouragement as well as receiving feedback she needs. For me, such input loses something when you have to ask for it, yet that is one way of teaching others how to encourage.

When you speak words that touch a chord in others, there is a counterreaction, and the reward comes when they choose to respond directly to you.

When others relay to you the concrete, positive changes taking place in their lives because of your encouragement, the elation you feel is incomparable. It is exhilarating to think you can actually play a part in altering another person's life for the better. There is also satisfaction in knowing that you have obeyed the command of God to "encourage one another."

SATISFACTION IN OBEYING GOD

In no way can we measure our Christian walk by what we do or don't do for God. What matters is who we are on the inside. That's one reason why encouraging others is so exciting. Not only are we obeying God, but we ourselves are changing on the inside as we do it. Every time we look for and see the good in others, we become less conscious of ourselves and our personal needs. We can't be caught up in our own problems and focus on other people at the same time. It's an either/or situation.

In coming to God, we understand that He never requires of us anything we're not capable of performing. He is the Great Enabler. When we hear His voice and realize we are supposed to be moving in a certain direction, He outfits us with the proper tools and equipment to perform the task— if we're standing still and not squirming around trying to get out of it.

Most children, as much as they balk and complain, obtain personal pleasure in obeying their parents. No matter how unpleasant the task, a certain satisfaction comes with knowing you've pleased those in authority over you. "... he who sows righteousness reaps a sure reward" (Prov. 11:18).

Whenever you encourage someone, you are sowing righteousness simply by being obedient to God. And there is a sense of immediate gratification because you've done what was asked of you by your heavenly Father.

RECIPROCATION

If you have established yourself as an encourager, it will usually follow that those around you will lift you up when you are in need as you did them. We learn by example. Whenever you encourage, you're teaching the recipient how to be an encourager.

I've watched certain Bible study teachers for a number of years, and I've observed that those who are lifestyle encouragers have definitely taught those who have sat in their classes to be the same. I believe the principle of "sowing and reaping" is activated in encouraging others.

As a free-lance writer, I teach writing classes and try to help new writers establish themselves in the profession. In any new area, beginners fumble along at the onset. These writers are no exception—it's the three-steps-forward/two-steps-back syndrome. They need lots and lots of encouragement along the way.

During one particular class I was teaching, I myself was thinking about quitting the whole business. I know of no writer who does not periodically threaten to quit—to leave the whole discouraging routine of writer's block, rejection slips, and the like.

This time I felt my frustration so intensely, I confessed it to my class, something I normally wouldn't do. I moaned and groaned for several minutes until suddenly one of my students piped up with, "How dare you think about quitting! Look at how far you've come. I'd give anything to be where you are. We're struggling just to get started and you're sitting there telling us you want to give up what we're trying so hard to achieve. I can't believe it!"

She looked totally disgusted with me, and I slunk down in my chair, feeling like an ungrateful wretch. (Another kick-in-the-pants encourager. Just what I need.) That's what we get for encouraging. It comes back to us full force. As we lift up others, we will be lifted up.

Not long after this little episode, I sold my first book. I haven't considered quitting since. But if it hadn't been for my student's encouraging words, I might have given it all up.

Jesus prayed and in the process taught His disciples to pray. Jesus healed, and His disciples learned to heal. Jesus preached, and His disciples preached. As we encourage, our "disciples" will encourage.

ENDEARING QUALITIES

The encouragers I know are deeply loved by not a few, but many. People love to be around them. Encouragers often exhibit other likeable character traits that cause people to be drawn to them. Possibly the act of encouraging has results in their developing such positive attributes as kindness, unselfishness, assertiveness, and confidence. To be an encourager means forever reaching outside of oneself toward others. How could one consistently move toward others and remain selfish or grumpy?

People today need so badly to be lifted up that they migrate in large numbers to anyone who will dole out support. And the encourager loves to provide what they need. It's not a matter of trying to "win friends and influence people," but if you want to encourage as many people as you can, it's definitely an asset to have folks drawn to you.

It's also a tremendous responsibility. You may feel a heavy incumbency as you attempt to carry those who look to you for encouragement. You may find yourself in a real grind of thinking you have to be continually "up," just in case someone needs you. However, if the objects of your encouragement never see you in a state of disheartenment, they will think you are Superperson and won't be able to relate wholeheartedly to you.

If you've always wondered what it is about some people that others are drawn to, look more closely now. Yes, some fortunate souls are born with charismatic personalities. But for many, it's the nature of Jesus Christ shining through them that makes them warm and personable.

SEEING ENCOURAGEMENT MULTIPLY

As we encourage, so will those around us encourage among themselves. One encourager I know is always touching and hugging everyone. As I observe those close to her, I see them move toward others in much the same way. They're a big bunch of cuddly teddy bears; you never saw such a lovey group. Incidentally, it works similarly when a leader is cold or standoffish—the rest of the group will follow suit.

It's not unusual for the encourager to hear his or her words used by one person to encourage another person. If you've fallen into the negative habit of criticizing others, you'll feel shame beyond belief to hear your words repeated. But then, if you're a criticizer, you probably won't recognize your words. Most criticizers don't realize what they're doing. If they did, I would hope that they would try to change.

When you're encouraging, you're sowing positive seeds in others' lives—seeds that, in most cases, will eventually sprout and bloom, sending forth a fragrant aroma what will touch many more lives than you can imagine. When you are around certain individuals on a regular basis, what is in you becomes part of them, which in turn becomes part of many others. Like an eddy of water moves from the inner circle, causing ripples all around it, so do you as an encourager affect many people around you. Every time you encourage one person, you make another wave. And when that person encourages the various people in his or her life, still another wave is created—until there is a powerful vortex of strong positive input flowing ceaselessly in its wake.

What a reward to know you can be such a powerful influence for good and create such a positive agitation in your little corner of the world.

ALL-AROUND GROWTH FOR YOU

The more you encourage, the more mature you become. You can't help but grow as you reach outside of yourself toward others.

For example, you are hurting, but someone needs you. As you lay aside your pain to encourage another person, you grow. Anytime we deny ourselves, we grow. Knowing I have to pull my own act together because others look to me for encouragement causes me to move much more quickly than I normally would. I might wallow around in my pit for quite a while if I knew no one was waiting for me, depending on me.

Growth happens as you learn to express your feelings for others through encouraging them. For some, this is not very difficult. For others, it can be a big step and agony all the way.

Growth continues as you learn to commit yourself to others on a long-term basis. Maintaining an effective level of encouragement over a period of time requires patience and steadfastness on your part, neither of which come easy for me. How about you?

Since I fear rejection, I grow each time I reach out to touch or hug someone. Of course, some people are easier to hug than others. With certain ones, I really have to stretch myself. But I feel better knowing that they do, too.

We are in this thing together. We encourage each other and we both grow. If you make yourself available, I'll encourage you. If you hide from me, I can't help you. Let's not rob each other of the growth God intends for us as we touch one another's lives. You will always grow through encouraging others whenever they can make themselves vulnerable and place themselves in a position to be built up.

WATCHING GROWTH IN OTHERS

Being able to observe the growth in those we encourage may just be the grand prize and number one reward for us as encouragers. Nothing quite matches the satisfaction and fulfillment we experience from watching positive changes take place in others as a result of our support and our words of upbuilding.

While teaching a weekly Bible study, I was privileged to see this happen many times. I would teach on a subject one week, we would discuss it, and the next week the women would return to report the results of their application of the teaching. A teacher's greatest reward is to watch those who "hear" really apply the teaching to their lives and, in turn, teach others. The same is true for encouragers who, in a sense, are teachers, also. Their greatest reward comes when those they encourage become encouragers themselves.

Encouragement is a valuable resource for the giver as well as the receiver. And many rewards await those who choose to live the life of an encourager.

If you saw in the newspaper that someone was offering a hundred-dollar reward for a lost briefcase you had found and now held in your possession, would you be anxious to collect? Of course, you would. Likewise, you will want to enjoy the serendipity that comes to you as an encourager—the eternal treasures that bring growth and satisfaction.

TIME TO CONSIDER

1. As you encourage, so will you be encouraged. Have you found your encouragement returning to you at times? How?

2. As an encourager, do you feel the pressure or responsibility to be "up" all the time? How can you relax and let Jesus shine through you?

3. As you've laid aside your personal pain to encourage someone else, have you grown? How?

4. Have you ever experienced God's enablement? Has He ever given you gifts or words of encouragement for others beyond what you know you personally have to offer? What were they?

9
...

How to Encourage Yourself

David commanded his soul to praise the Lord. In Psalms 103 and 104 he repeated the phrase, "Praise the Lord, O my soul" five times. David knew how to encourage himself in the Lord. Praise builds up our inner selves.

It would be wonderful if we could always depend on one another for encouragement. Unfortunately, we all suffer those extremely lonely times when no one is in close proximity and we are sinking emotionally. What do we do?

In the same way that we build up others, we can build up ourselves. However, it's not easy, for when you're feeling low, you have very little strength to minister to yourself. But it can be done. Following are some suggestions that I hope will help you next time you're feeling discouraged.

LIST YOUR BLESSINGS

It's difficult to stay in the pits when you begin to count all the positives in your life. Take basic needs for instance: food in your cupboard, running water from the tap, a warm bed at night, even a roof over your head. When I read in the daily newspaper about the hundreds of homeless and hungry people in my own city, I realize that my home and my food are truly things for which I can be thankful. Friendships, health, children, and jobs are other things for which we can be thankful. Not to mention hobbies and activities that give us pleasure as well as good music and books.

You may be one of those whose basic needs are not being met. Your job may have been terminated recently, or your friends might have deserted you. Your pain is real and cannot be underestimated.

However, in the worst of situations, if I can find even one or two things for which to be thankful, my perspective begins to change. Although your problems continue, the advantage is that you can think more clearly about how to deal with them if you're not an emotional mess.

When my freezer in the garage was broken into and $250 worth of beef stolen, I was thankful the culprits did not also decide to break into the house where we were sleeping. We can always find something to be thankful for if we look hard enough.

Don't get the wrong idea. I ranted and raved plenty before I became thankful. I obviously haven't perfected this thing yet.

Paul wrote, "Be joyful always," and "give thanks in all circumstances" in the same clause. Giving thanks causes the joy of the Lord to surge forth, even in what seem impossible circumstances.

If you can cease focusing on the one or two things wrong with your life and redirect your vision to the many things right with it, you are encouraging yourself—and the healing process can begin.

BE CAREFUL OF THE COMPANY YOU KEEP

When you're feeling discouraged, it's wise to pay careful attention to the people with whom you spend time. If you keep company with those who are also in a wretched state of mind, you'll only feed one another's discontent. You'll both spout a lot of negative allegations you'll later wish you could retract. Since neither of you is in a condition to help anyone, you'll both come away feeling worse than before, having done nothing for each other but exchange negative charges.

On the other hand, it's not advantageous to be around someone who is super-happy either. If you're crying, you'd like the world to cry with you. It makes you angry to see the rest of the world laugh while you cry.

There are certain individuals in my life on whom I can depend to be whatever it is I need them to be at any given time. If I'm crying, they'll cry with me, if I'm laughing, they'll laugh with me. They are the ones I migrate toward, whatever my mood.

I don't want to be a stumbling block to a weaker Christian. Therefore, sometimes when I'm feeling discouraged in a resentful sort of way, I unplug my phone, for fear that I might damage someone who may be easily influenced by my attitude. You see, this principle works both ways. So encourage yourself when you're down by either avoiding the wrong kind of folks or surrounding yourself with the right kind.

FOCUS ON A LARGER VISION

I can sink awfully low before I am forced to remind myself that God's vision for me is so much larger than my present trouble. In actuality, the trouble may be large, but it will seem puny when compared to the purpose for which God has called me, whatever it may be at the moment.

God is all-wise and has big plans for His children. Unfortunately, while God's vision of our lives is a grand panorama, we humans only "see through a glass darkly."

What seems large to us may be small to Him and vice versa. The point is, many Christians and non-Christians alike live and die without ever seeing God's vision for them completed. This happens because we allow ourselves to become so consumed with our troubles. "A righteous man may have many troubles, but the Lord delivers him from them all" (Ps. 34:19). The Lord will take care of our problems if we can just look beyond them. Since troubles will always be with us, it's up to us to keep ourselves from being devoured by them. If we can consistently focus on the master blueprint and commit to God the worrisome disconcertions of that blueprint, we will begin to see our dreams and goals accomplished. Outside the walls of our complicated and at times neurotic lives exists a hopeless world that needs us. Step outside those walls that imprison you and catch a glimpse of the larger picture.

FOCUS ON ETERNITY

"This too will pass" is a favorite saying of many. And it usually does. When we line up our causes for discouragement and balance them against what matters eternally, we might find that less matters than we previously thought.

How much difference does it make that your washing

machine broke down today and a repair man can't come before next week?

How much does it matter that your son broke his finger and can't play basketball the rest of the season? His disappointment can't be minimized, but in light of eternity, does it make a huge difference?

If we will fully realize we're going to live forever, what seems monumentally important will become insignificant. The excruciating pain of the moment can later be used to encourage someone else down the road, and even the cause of our pain is often of mere temporal importance.

We humans are fairly resilient when it comes right down to it. We heal from heartbreaking divorces, a loved one's death, abuse by other people. We not only heal, but we rise to our feet and move on.

Looking at life from an eternal perspective, God and people are all that matter. In encouraging yourself, examine carefully the cause for your discouragement and ask yourself if it will make an eternal difference. Will today's source of discouragement matter in eternity? Jesus said we should store up for ourselves treasures in heaven—tomorrow will worry about itself (Matt. 6:20, 34).

DO SOMETHING WORTHWHILE

Encourage yourself by doing something worthwhile. It might be mowing the lawn or making a special dessert for dinner or whatever *you* think is worthwhile. Yardwork is fulfilling for me because my time schedule does not permit me to work outside as often as I'd like. Consequently, when I do, it makes a big difference in both the exterior of my home and how I feel inside.

When you're down, it's amazing what a little physical activity will do. For you, it might be painting a picture or playing golf. I jump rope every day for exercise, and even the worst of situations looks less terrible by the time I'm done.

Doing something worthwhile for someone else can also distract you from your own troubles. In his book *How to Be a People Helper,* Dr. Gary Collins, professor of psychology, explains it this way:

> Sometimes activity is the best therapy. Alcoholics Anonymous discovered this many years ago and developed a successful rehabilitation program, in which people with a drinking problems help each other.
>
> Many of us are probably guilty of what has been called the gold-rush syndrome. In gold-rush days the prospector didn't dare stop to help another man who might be having trouble. To do so was to lose time, and then someone else, maybe even the man he stopped to help, might beat him out for the best claim. The result was a highly individualized, self-centered, private existence. Like the men who passed by the wounded traveler before the Good Samaritan came along, we hurry through life, engrossed in our own little worlds and perhaps bearing our own burdens. We push toward our own goals and fail to realize that to help another person has great therapeutic value for ourselves. This isn't the only solution to our problems, but when we help somebody else we often get the greatest benefit ourselves.[1]

Getting moving when we are discouraged not only distracts us from our problems, but we automatically feel better because we have accomplished something of value.

Motivating yourself to move is the most difficult part of it. If your activity is something that vaguely resembles work, promise yourself a reward when the job is completed. For example, sit down later and read a book without feeling guilty. Oftentimes I become so involved in my project that I forget to stop and reward myself. The feeling of satisfaction in a job well done is reward enough.

If you don't feel like tackling a project, take a step toward it anyway. The motivation will usually follow.

GIVE YOURSELF TIME

We can encourage ourselves by learning not to rush through the process of emotions. When we find ourselves in the midst of emotional ordeals such as broken relationships or grief, the emotional process involved should be left to run its natural course. However, if we choose to drag it out beyond this point, we risk developing bitterness, rage, or some other poisonous emotion.

I remember going to bed once and feeling the urge to cry for the eighty-seventh time that day. I also knew intuitively that if I cried over this particular situation one more time I would fall into a terrible depression. I decided not to cry and by morning the burden was lifted.

Sometimes, when life seems absolutely unbearable, I play a little game with myself. By the time my discouragement approaches this point, I'm usually a mess and have nothing to lose. I know I really do need to get on with life. That's when I decide to sit down and hurt for five minutes and *only* five minutes. I look at my watch and then dive into intense self-pity.

"Oh, this hurts. What she said to me was really rotten. Life is so unfair. I hate myself. Ouch! Why does everything happen to me? No one loves me. . ." and so on and so on, ad nauseam. I never exceed the time limit. This may sound crazy, but it usually works—and I'm for anything that works when depression is taking that much energy.

READ AND MEDITATE ON SCRIPTURE

We can also encourage ourselves by reading and meditating on Scripture. I realize that I risk insulting your intelligence or your faith by even mentioning this. But I hope you will consider it a gentle reminder that the Word of God is a soothing antidote for discouragement.

Because I identify with David's suffering, I have worn out the Psalms section of my Bible. But a word of warning—be sure to let the Lord lead you to the scriptures that will comfort you in your situation. Otherwise, you could end up in dire straits. How? By reading such verses as, "then the Lord rained down burning sulfur on Sodom and Gomorrah. . . . But Lot's wife looked back and she became a pillar of salt" (Gen. 19:24, 26). Or, "The Egyptians were fleeing toward it, and the Lord swept them into the sea. . . . Not one of them survived" (Exod. 14:27, 28). These stories were included in the Bible for good reason, but personally I don't think God was thinking about your problems when He inspired Moses to write them. So, unless you want to end up really discouraged and believing God wants to kill you, don't meditate on these particular verses of Scripture while you're down.

Instead, read: "The Lord is close to the brokenhearted and saves those who are crushed in spirit" (Ps. 34:18). Or: "He will make your righteousness shine like the dawn, the justice of your cause like the noonday sun" (Ps. 37:6).

If you don't find a verse that comforts immediately, keep looking. God wants to encourage you, and He used men to write the Scriptures for that very reason, among many others. Be patient. Give the Lord time to direct you to what He wants you to read.

BE HONEST WITH GOD

Another way to encourage ourselves is to be honest with God. Don't try to hide your emotions from God. He can handle them. There is nothing He hasn't seen before or even experienced firsthand when He walked on earth. I'm a deep feeling person, and when I try to conceal my emotions from the Lord, it's like trying to hide an elephant in an open field. It took me many years of walking with God before I could believe that He wasn't going to punish me for my feelings.

Now, when I feel anger, I tell Him about it. God is even the object of my anger at times. No point in trying to hide it. Even if He couldn't read my thoughts He can see the frown creasing my brow as I pray. God has a lot to put up with in me. You know how some children get weepy when they are hurt and you want to cuddle them and hold them and kiss away the pain, and how others kick and scream and throw themselves on the floor and you want to send them to their rooms? That's me. I'm very reactive if I so much as stub my toe.

God doesn't wring His hands and break out in a sweat because I'm throwing myself around. Instead, He waits until I've worn myself out, then asks, "How can I help you?"

It doesn't work to deny our true emotions. Suppressing them only intensifies their power and delays the healing. It's as we become aware of our own pain and express it to God that He heals us.

RELEASE YOUR DISCOURAGEMENT TO GOD

After 'fessing up to the way we truly feel inside, we can let go of our hurt: "God, I can't carry this any longer. It's too heavy."

The Gift of Encouragement

If you were carrying a huge load of bricks down the street and a five-hundred-pound giant happened along and offered to carry them for you, would you refuse?—"No, thank you. I'd like to carry them awhile longer. I've grown used to them, and I really don't know what I'd do without them."

What a ridiculous scenario! Yet, in effect, that's what we are saying to God when we continue to carry our own burdens. At times we may even lack the strength to pray. But God knows our hearts even when we don't utter a word, and He'll take what's there and begin to build on it.

God hurts for His children. He hurts when you lose your job. He hurts when your son becomes dependent on drugs. He hurts when your spouse walks out on you. Yet, at a spirit level, He has power to comfort, to heal, to make it somehow bearable—if you'll trust Him with your pain.

DON'T COMPARE YOURSELF WITH OTHERS

Another type of self-encouragement comes when we learn to avoid comparing ourselves with others. Everyone is different. We all handle various degrees of pain in a myriad of ways. What hurts you may not even faze someone else. Here are a couple of examples of what I mean:

"Janey's husband went through open-heart surgery, too, and it didn't affect her family at all like it's affected us."

"Why should it bother me so much that Steve got that position instead of me? Roy was also in line for it, and he acts like he couldn't care less, just says he'll try again next time."

That explains why we can never truly say we "understand" another's pain. Because we really don't. Even if we experience similar traumas, our perceptions of pain and our responses to it are so varied that we can never fully comprehend another's suffering.

110

Don't look at Karen and assume that because she got over a heartbreaking divorce in three months and nineteen days it will be the same for you. It may take you from six months to a year, depending on the circumstances surrounding the breakup and on your own personality.

Do the best you can, stay open to the healing of the Holy Spirit, and try not to concern yourself with how someone else handled a similar situation.

THINGS WILL EVENTUALLY BE BETTER

"The Lord blessed the latter part of Job's life more than the first" (Job 42:12).

It is difficult to imagine while you're in the midst of trouble that things will ever be better. While Job was scraping his sores, he must have thought he would be doing that forever. I'm sure it must have seemed like forever at the time.

Pain, possibly emotional pain even more than physical pain, can be so devastating and poignant that we're sure it will kill us. That's why it is so important to keep a semblance of perspective. Suffering is only a momentary loss. Our lives can be restored to health or rebuilt, often sooner than we thought possible.

Self-encouragement is not easy. None of the methods discussed in this chapter will work for everyone 100 percent of the time. The important thing to know is that when no one (your pastor, a friend, a spouse) is available to build you up when you're discouraged, it is possible to encourage yourself in the presence of the Lord.

Encouraging yourself is often a matter of changing your thought patterns. If you can move your mind off your problems and onto practically anything else, you can begin the healing process. I'm not advocating that you not deal with your problems. Of course you should deal with the *source* of your discouragement. Do everything you know how to do, then move on to the next phase of your life.

I strongly believe that if we commit ourselves to becoming encouragers, not only to others but to ourselves, many of life's problems could be avoided entirely. I call it "preventive medicine."

TIME TO CONSIDER

1. What or who is the greatest source of discouragement in your life right now? Can this be changed? If not, how can you encourage yourself "in the midst of" the problem?

2. David encouraged himself in the Lord. Make a list of five things for which you can give God praise no matter how long your discouraging situation persists.

3. One way to encourage ourselves is to find purpose in our pain. From God's perspective, what is happening in your life? How is He developing His character in you through your pain?

4. "Give, and it will be given to you" (Luke 6:38). Think of at least three people who are in need at the moment. How could God use you to encourage them? What do you have to give?

5. Are you or God carrying your hurtful situation? How can you release it and then leave it where it belongs?

6. We get well one step at a time. Can you commit to "encourage yourself in the Lord" at least once a day? How will you begin?

10

...

Written Encouragement

A professor at a Bible college who was fresh out of seminary struggled to keep up with his lesson planning in unfamiliar material. One day, instead of starting his usual lecture, he asked for understanding and forgiveness of the students because of his poor preparation over the last few weeks. He also requested prayer for his workload.

Because of this professor's struggle, one of his students started an organization called the Barnabas Committee. Her name was Jeanne Doering, and she writes about it in an article entitled, "The Power of Encouragement," published in *Christian Herald*. Anonymously, the students began to send typed notes of encouragement to the faculty members, attaching gifts such as candy bars, apples, or animal crackers. These simple tokens of appreciation changed the entire atmosphere of the college campus.[1]

The Gift of Encouragement

The written form of encouragement is often over-looked. Yet a card, a note, or a letter expressing one's deepest heartfelt thoughts can work wonders for another.

How uplifting it is when I pick up my mail and find, among the bills and junk ads, an envelope addressed to me, especially when I discover it's not even a wedding or shower invitation, but a message of love and encouragement. These notes are not usually penned in flowery phrases or eloquent poetry. Instead, they are simple expressions of the heart.

You don't have to be an English major to write a note of encouragement to someone. Anyone can do it. If it's from the heart, the message will come through despite improper grammar, misspelled words, or illegible handwriting.

Recently I received the following note:

Dear Gloria:

I always enjoy talking to you on the phone. You really brighten my day. You always come across with this expression in your voice which says, "Hey, you are an important person and I'm so glad you called."

My friend went on to tell me many reasons for which she thanked God for our friendship. I cried at the end of it. I so needed some encouragement that day. Nobody had ever before told me they appreciated that about me.

You see, I strive to sound friendly on the phone. I answer with a chatty "hi" instead of a cordial "hello" so the people calling will know that I'm willing and ready (usually) to talk to them, that if they are thinking deeply enough about me to call, they deserve a friendly greeting.

On bad days when nothing seems to be going right, I'm often tempted to answer the phone with a grumpy abrupt "hello" all the while thinking, *What do you want?* Before I received my friend's note, I might have given in to that temptation if I thought no one would notice the difference. But now when the phone rings, I am able to lay my problems temporarily aside, so the person on the other end of the line won't have to regret calling.

What if my friend hadn't written? I don't know about you, but I cringe when someone answers the phone with a mean-sounding hello! I take the affront personally, even though I realize that the person on the other end of the phone doesn't even know who I am yet. So because someone noticed that I am friendly on the phone and took the time to acknowledge it, I now make the extra effort on those days cheeriness doesn't come naturally.

Why a note? Wouldn't it be just as effective—and easier—to pick up the phone and dial? Or convey the message the next time we meet? Perhaps. But writing may be a better way for some situations, and it need not be a chore, as we shall see.

WHY WRITE IT?

Reasons for writing notes abound. I hope the following few will convince you that the next time a name passes through your mind, it may be because the Lord would have you write that person a note of encouragement.

• A note may prove the most efficient means of conveying what you're feeling for someone. Because the person is not standing in front of you weighing your every word, you can take as much time as you need to think exactly what it is you want to say. You can edit, scratch out, and write as many rough drafts as you choose until it satisfies you.

• Because you won't be present to see it, you don't have to anticipate any particular reaction on the part of the receiver. This can be an advantage if you are the type of person who can accomplish a "hello," but who gets tongue-tied in the succeeding minutes.

• Although thoughts of encouragement may come at any time, they most often occur when you're somewhere other than in the presence of the person about whom you're thinking. The thought may be so fleeting, you let it drift off without mentally nailing it down. And when this happens, the one who needs to hear it never does. But if you can sit down and write a note while the thought is still fresh on your mind, what might have been only a fleeting impulse, ending up nowhere, becomes instead an encouraging message to brighten someone's life.

• The receiver can read a note or card at his or her convenience. Unlike a telephone call, which may interrupt something important, a card breezes into the home with the rest of the mail and will lie there as long as is necessary, never demanding to be opened like the ringing phone demands to be answered.

• The written form of encouragement can be filed away for future reference. I've often wished my brain was a computer, so I could recall many of the kind words with which others have blessed me through the years. I'm thankful for those who have chosen to write theirs down, for many have been the days when I needed to pull out the box full of encouraging notes and cards (I don't save the mean ones), reminding me that I'm a person with value, that someone somewhere loves me even if I don't love myself at the moment.

KEEP SUPPLIES ON HAND

You'll discover you are much more likely to write if you have the necessary supplies at your disposal. Nothing kills the desire quicker than realizing you don't have a stamp, an envelope, or a decent piece of paper.

I always keep on hand one or two books of stamps and anywhere from five to ten different kinds of notecards, both serious and humorous. (I have one set of cards now that shows the contents of a taco on the front. The flap that folds around it is the taco shell.) You can find in any stationery store a great assortment of cards to meet your particular needs.

You might want to keep some specialized cards on hand for occasions such as birthdays and anniversaries. That way, when someone's special day sneaks up on you, you won't have to make a trip to the store. A birthday card provides you the perfect opportunity to encourage someone. A few personal words added to the printed message gives any commercial card a special touch.

HOW-TO'S

In discussing how-to's, I'm really inclined to say, "Just sit down and do it." But there are a few tips that can make your written encouragement more effective.

If you are lifting up a person in an area you know to be a weak one, ask the Lord to show you a Scripture verse to include in your note. Our own words seem so inadequate at times and incapable of reaching deep enough to touch a person's hurt. Scripture will accomplish what our humanness cannot. It will heal, bring forgiveness, reveal the depth of God's love.

An encouraging note should be kept short and to the point for maximum impact. It loses its punch when it rambles on and on in redundancy. The first paragraph states the specific purpose for the note, the second paragraph expands on that purpose, the last paragraph wraps it up and says "good-bye."

A WRITING MINISTRY

If you find you derive real pleasure from writing out your thoughts and feelings, you might want to ask the Lord to use your writing in active ministry for Him. Many people are isolated from the outside world and would benefit greatly from your notes of encouragement.

Prisoners, for example, rarely get enough encouragement. I've been corresponding with a young inmate at the state penitentiary for over two years now. Other than his wife, who is not much of a writer, I'm the only person he hears from in a positive way. He has even received hate mail from angry relatives who are using his imprisonment as an opportunity to tell him what a jerk they've always thought he was. This young man is in desperate need of encouragement. If he doesn't hear from me for a month, I receive a letter begging me to please write. What else does he have to look forward to in the immediate future?

It always amazes me that my letters, as shallow as I feel they may be at times, are so treasured and truly a source of life to this prisoner. He is typical of thousands of such prisoners across the land. We may be their only contact with warm, loving human beings. I would wager a guess that the guards and other inmates aren't all that warm, loving, or touchable!

When we write to prisoners, we especially need to keep our letters upbeat and full of hope. Behind the iron bars that disconnect the prison population from the rest of humanity lies of world or violence, hate, and turmoil. An outsider may be their only source of good news. A prisoner who is the victim of daily negative input may fast become hardened to the real world. From his vantage point, it is easy to believe that everyone is out to get him, that self-preservation is man's highest goal, and that any

118

type of behavior is permissible in order to survive.

To counteract this process, I believe my letters to my friend in prison instill hope for his future, reinforce my belief in him as a person, and remind him that someone in the real world still thinks about him, loves him, and prays for him. Take on a personal challenge to make a prisoner laugh. Send a cartoon, write a funny story, relate a joke.

Missionaries are another whole group of people who need encouraging mail. They work long hard hours in faraway lands and can easily feel forgotten if they do not receive letters from home to uplift them. Too often we view missionaries only as spiritual towers of strength, giving their lives for the natives of another country and—because of God's anointing—trucking on, day after day, always smiling, never downhearted, tired, or discouraged.

Or we don't think about them at all.

Missionaries are human. They are physically isolated, perhaps preaching the gospel to jungle natives who care little whether or not the missionaries are there, or who may even be openly hostile. They're separated from family, friends, and even America itself with all the modern comforts to which they have grown accustomed. Missionaries need to be encouraged. They long to hear about last week's Bible study, this week's potluck, next week's special evangelist. They need to know you're praying for them, that their lives are appreciated.

Passing a note is another effective method of ministering in writing. I realize that this is something we teach our children *not* to do. And without too much effort, we ourselves can evoke memories from the past of getting caught passing notes in school and the forthcoming penalty for such criminal activity. But there are times when this form of encouragement can be extremely effective. Once when I was feeling insecure with a certain friend, she passed me a note during church that reaffirmed our friendship. She simply wrote the words: "Love is patient, love is kind. It does not envy, it does not boast, it is not proud. It is not rude, it is not self-seeking. Love does not delight in evil but rejoices with the truth. It always protects, always trusts, always hopes, always perseveres" (1 Cor. 13:4–7).

But that's all it took. As the service continued, I let those words sink into my spirit, realizing anew the depth of not only God's love, but the love of His children also. I rested secure. I have kept the note to remind me of what I learned that day, along with another note I once received that simply said: "You look beautiful today."

How much I cherish these touches of encouragement. Now I always keep a special notepad in my purse for those occasions in church or other meetings when I want to express my appreciation for someone spontaneously.

I'm not advocating regular correspondence during church services, lest your pastor (or mine) get the wrong idea. But occasions do present themselves when a note passed down the row (not across the aisle) will be just what someone needs.

Know that your note or letter is appreciated at the time it's read. Although most people will let you know what it did for them, some will forget to acknowledge that they even received it. That may be because of the time lapse between when they read it and when they see you, or it's possible they are at a loss for what to say, so they say nothing.

The purpose of sending notes of encouragement is not so that we will be blessed, but so we may bless others. Your note will be read, and read again, then treasured for a long time to come—if my experience is representative of most recipients of appreciation notes.

One final word of caution. Don't cop out by writing a

note when you should say it in person. A note can be an efficacious means of encouragement, but it's not a substitute for the much needed personal touch found in face-to-face contact.

I have an evasive friend who goes to great lengths to avoid direct contact and who rarely reaches out. I once received a note from her when I was hurting. As much as I appreciated it, I remember thinking, *Oh, how I wish she'd touch me, hold me.* I knew she was taking the easy way out because she was dodging personal contact. Admittedly, at certain times it's more convenient, or perhaps less "embarrassing," to sit down and write a note to someone who really needs to feel your arms around her. But it's difficult to feel that physical touch through a piece of paper.

As we learn to be sensitive to when a note would be welcome, we must also learn to recognize when not to put our thoughts in writing.

Still, a written message is a tangible expression of love, and—in a day when absolutes seem so elusive and realities slip between our fingers—how much we need something we can see, hold on to, something that gives life meaning. Your written words represent you—your time and your love for others.

TIME TO CONSIDER

1. How can notes, cards, and letters often encourage in a way that verbal encouragement can't?

2. How does it make you feel when someone takes the time to write you a note of encouragement? What does it communicate?

3. Think of someone in your life for whom you've been praying. If you were to write a note of encouragement to

The Gift of Encouragement

this person, what do you think the Lord would want you to write? Include a Scripture verse and why you feel it meets a need at this particular time.

11

...

Verbal Encouragement

Verbal encouragement is absolutely essential for the health and well-being of one's spirit. We must hear with an inner ear words from others that tell us why we make a significant difference in the world in which we live.

Words can tear down. Words can build up.

Words can crush. Words can heal.

Words can kill. Words can give life.

"The tongue has the power of life and death . . ." (Prov. 18:21).

In her dynamic book, *You Are Not the Target,* Laura Archer Huxley cites an instance of a woman about to undergo surgery.

The surgery is not serious, but the patient is apprehensive, and drowsy from sedatives. A well-meaning

123

comforter reassures her: "Don't worry, dear—it will all be over in less than two hours." What can be wrong with that? For the conscious mind it would probably be reassuring. But the conscious mind is not quite there; illness and anxiety have left the field open to the subconscious mind, and this takes whatever is said with the utmost literalness. "It will all be over in less than two hours!" So far as the subconscious mind is concerned, it means that in less than two hours it will be all over with her—she will be dead! All over . . . all over . . . it is with this dismal and debilitating thought that she goes to the operating room.[1]

Fortunately this woman expressed her fear to the anesthetist, who immediately understood and counteracted it with careful and comforting reassurance.

Ms. Huxley goes on to explain:

All good anesthetists are aware nowadays of the power of words on anxious semiconscious and even on completely unconscious patients. It is now generally accepted that the perception of sound persists long after the perception of pain has been anesthetized . . . surgery is a special case of mental and physical stress. To a lesser degree the same principle holds in other stressful situations such as painful emotions, exhaustion, sickness and shock.[2]

We must carefully consider how our words will influence other people, whether they will destroy or bring life. The virtuous woman "speaks with wisdom, and faithful instruction is on her tongue" (Prov. 31:26).

One of my first recollections of someone encouraging me was a casual remark made some time after I'd spoken publicly for a total of maybe five minutes at a large women's gathering. Referring to my impromptu speech, one woman said, "I never knew you were so funny."

Funny? Me? The conversation continued around me, but this woman's words clung to my spirit, fitting snugly around it like a wool cardigan in sub-zero temperatures. As I recalled the evening she referred to, I remember the laughter all right, but at the time I was unaware of what provoked it. All I really remembered was my struggle to communicate a concept, and the more I talked, the more the audience laughed. I was pleased they were enjoying my little talk, but it wasn't supposed to be a comedy routine. Afterwards I had walked away slightly frustrated, feeling that I had failed to put my message across.

Now this woman was telling me I was funny. I had always suffered extreme self-consciousness and lack of confidence, rarely speaking out in a group situation. But if I could make people laugh, apparently I had a sense of humor that had been lying dormant. Now it appeared to be an asset.

I began to speak out more and noticed that my words oftentimes did evoke laughter in others. With each laugh I gained confidence because the response of the audience seemed to express acceptance of me as a person.

I never strove to be funny. If it happened, it happened. I couldn't help it. Now I have to keep a lid on my humor because I can find something funny about everything and everybody.

Because of this dear woman's words, I was set free in an area of my personality that had previously been bound. Her words changed my life and strongly affected the way I relate to others.

Now that we're aware of the tongue as such a powerful tool, how can we best use it to bring life to others?

CONQUER FEAR

The first step in encouraging others is to conquer the fear of how we're going to come across or how what we are saying is going to be received. If we can convince ourselves that it really doesn't matter, we'll be well on our way.

And it really *doesn't* matter. The object of encouragement is not to prove to ourselves or anyone else how well we can articulate. Nor is it to receive a big smile and a "Thank you—you're so wonderful" from the recipient of our encouragement.

The purpose of encouragement is to build up another person. Lest we lose sight of that objective, we must overcome our fear of something that, in actuality, is of little significance in light of our broader goal.

"The one who is in you is greater than the one who is in the world" (1 John 4:4). Because Jesus, the Author of encouragement in us, is greater than Satan, the author of fear, ". . . we are more than conquerors through him who loved us" (Rom. 8:37). This is the only verse in the Bible in which the word *conquerors* is used—the Greek word is *hupernikao*, meaning "to vanquish beyond," to gain a decisive victory.

The only method I know for gaining victory is to face the enemy. To run is to surrender. Every time we advance on the enemy, fear, we gain new territory. The truth is, it will not be long until you will barely remember the fear of approaching others with encouragement. And you certainly will not be able to understand how you could have been afraid of such a rewarding experience.

In deciding to gain victory over my fear, we need to hold in front of us the proverbial carrot-in-front-of-the-donkey. In this case, it's not what we will gain, but what others will lose if we remain in our fearful state.

You are needed. Because of the unique places you've walked and the personal trials you've suffered and your fresh perspective on life's experiences, you can offer what no one else can. So don't allow fear or self-consciousness to stop you from motivating others, from pushing them onward and upward, from moving them closer to God.

APPROACH

After you've conquered fear, the next thing to know is that your approach can be of some consequence in how your encouragement is received. I have emphasized that you should not *worry* about how your words are received. This is true only as long as you're not the one responsible for lack of reception. If you're too pushy in your approach or too wishy-washy, you won't be taken seriously.

Eye contact is especially important. When your eyes connect with another person's eyes, know you have that person's full attention.

KEEP IT SHORT

"A man of knowledge uses words with restraint . . ." (Prov. 17:27).

Unless you are giving a eulogy, it's best to keep your praise short and to the point. A few sentences should do it. This way you won't embarrass the one you're praising. An exception to this rule is a situation where you're encouraging someone who is hurting and who wants to dialogue with you. You may have to repeat yourself a number of times before you convince such individuals of their value or that the Lord is in control of their particular situation or need.

Under normal circumstances, though, keeping it short will maximize the impact of your words. If you go on at great length, it will begin to sound like adulation, even if that is not your intent.

TONE OF VOICE

The tone of your voice is a significant factor in expressing encouragement. Your words may say one thing, but your tone can convey an entirely different message.

I remember a grueling project a friend and I were once working on together. Into our fourth year on this thing, she had at last finished her part. When I finally completed mine, I called her up and, so excited I could hardly contain myself, screamed, "I'm done! I'm done! I'm done! D-O-N-E! Can you believe it?"

There was a pause from the other end of the line, then, "Oh, that's nice," in a flat tone of voice that implied either it was about time or she didn't think it was nice at all.

My balloon of accomplishment immediately deflated because of her tone of voice.

When we discussed it later, I discovered she had a good reason for her lack of enthusiasm. She had enjoyed working with me on this project and would miss our times together. She feared we would seldom see each other anymore.

I could handle that. With her fresh words of encouragement, she pumped my balloon back up again.

You may be saying one thing, but your true feelings, revealed through your tone of voice, may be expressing something completely different. For example, you can casually tell your spouse, "I love you." Or you can look intensively into your loved one's eyes and utter those same words in your most seductive voice, so that they mean: "I wish I could tell you how much I really love you."

In both instances, your actual words are identical, but the tone of your voice is the distinguishing characteristic conveying their meaning. When we encourage, we need to do it as though we mean it—or we might as well not do it at all.

People are special and should be treated as such. Your tone of voice can convey your enthusiasm over their specialness, or it can imply rejection.

When the doorbell rings and you open the door, does your tone of voice advertise your true feelings?

If a salesman toting a briefcase is standing there, your "hello" might sound like: "What do *you* want?"

If it is your chatty neighbor next door, your "hello" might reveal: "Oh, boring . . . give me a break."

If you opened the door to greet a casual acquaintance, your "hello" might mean: "How nice. Come in."

If it is a dear friend, your "hello" would say: "All right! I'm so glad you came over. Can't think of anyone else I'd rather see."

When I walk through heaven's gate, I expect that Someone will be there to greet me, and I hope that same Someone will be excited to see me, glad I made it, after all.

Wouldn't it be wonderful if we could depend on such a warm welcome from one another down here? Well, why not?

"Look who's here! I'm so glad to see you. Won't you come into my life and sit down?" That is what your tone of voice can convey, and it should, if you want to be an encourager.

YOUR STYLE

As in all that you do, your encouragement will carry its own unique flavor. Be comfortable with whatever it turns out to be, and let it develop out of your personality. Be yourself.

When I was first learning about encouragement, I would

watch this friend of mine and try to emulate her. In listening to others' hurts, she would get this sad look on her face and frequently mumble, "Ohhh," throughout the other person's woes. She would *always* say, "I love you," and *always* offer to pray. It was inconceivable for her to end any encounter without a hug. That was her style, her personality. By nature she is a compassionate person.

It wasn't long before I realized that in my attempts to be like her, I was moving farther away from being me. It's not my style to *always* say, "I love you." Sometimes it is. I try to remember, but I often forget to pray, and much of the time hugging never even enters into my realm of thinking.

So, in being me, what do I do? I usually ask a lot of questions. I'm also finding it easier to empathize with others, and my empathy may lead me to say, "I'm so sorry. How can I help you?" Or it may evoke a tear. Or I might say or do nothing at all.

The important thing is that I be me, for in being me, the caring you see is real. Unfortunately, my encouragement may be served on a paper plate instead of dished out on a silver platter like my friend's. My tears may only half fill a paper cup with encouragement while my friend's tears overflow a crystal goblet. I may not say what you want me to say or in the way you want me to say it.

But I'll try my best, not because I want to be known as "The Most Encouraging Person," but because I care about you.

PHONE CALLS

The telephone can be such a nuisance at times that I could easily rip it out of the wall, silencing forever its incessant ringing. Other times I curse it for not ringing because I so desperately need to hear from someone who loves me.

Many are the times I have picked up the receiver to see if the dial tone was still buzzing. I was sure the phone must be out of order; it had been so long since I had heard the longed for ding-a-ling-a-ling.

It finally rings. I rush to answer. Someone is thinking about me. "Hello!" I answer breathlessly.

"Mrs. Chisholm, this is the Cheery Chipper Congenial Carpet Cleaning Service. We'll be in your area. . . ." The calculated voice of the caller screeches to an abrupt halt as I say, "Thanks, but no thanks."

For fear of "bothering" one another, we seldom even obey the impulse to make short encouraging phone calls just to say "I love you" and "I'm thinking about you." How long does it take to say that? One minute, maybe two at the most.

I think I could possibly drag myself away from my vacuum cleaner or my washing machine to hear that you love me. Now that I think about it, there's not anything I wouldn't put down to hear a few words of encouragement. "Bother" me any time.

It's always a good idea to inquire of the person you're calling as to whether or not it's a convenient time for them to talk. A "friend" called me at eleven-thirty one night and without asking if I was busy or in bed launched into a lengthy discourse about all the events in her life during the last week or so. It was not a good time for me to talk, even if it had been an encouraging phone call, which it wasn't.

Sometimes I'll be standing in the kitchen cooking dinner and start thinking about someone. Then I decide to make a spontaneous phone call for no other reason than to say, "I love you and I'm so glad you're in my life."

131

GIVING ADVICE VERSUS OFFERING SUGGESTIONS

Advice is the giving of one's opinion as to what to do or how to handle a situation. A *suggestion* is the mentioning of something to think over or act on. There's a big difference between the two—the difference between "you should . . ." and "why don't you think about . . ."—in short, the difference between preaching and encouraging.

I respond much better to the second one, unless I'm at my wit's end and by my own volition, *choose* to lie on the psychiatrist's couch.

It's so easy to give advice, to tell others what they should or shouldn't do, what you would do if you were in their shoes. It's much more difficult to withhold your personal judgments on another's situation than to pose questions that may help that person decide on his or her own what would be the best course of action.

When others do ask you for advice (which is seldom the case, unless you are a paid counselor), it would behoove you to take your time answering. No off-the-cuff response for another person's life. We get ourselves in enough personal trouble without also getting those around us in trouble.

When someone is in need of help and you can see past the obstacles in his or her path, you can offer solid suggestions without dogma:

"Have you thought about. . . ?"

"Let's consider your alternatives. . . ."

"Why not try. . . ?"

"Are you sure about. . . ?"

After all your suggestions have been made and considered, let your final offer be: "No matter what you decide, I'll be there."

132

OFFER TO PRAY VERBALLY

"When all else fails, pray" seems to be the prevailing attitude among many of us, myself included, when actually it should be our first course of action, so that we have enough wisdom to offer constructive help.

Why verbal prayer? Can't we pray silently? And do we have to pray in the presence of others?

There are three good reasons why praying aloud, so that others can listen to our words, is an effective form of encouragement.

1. We pray aloud for others because we want them to be able to hear our petition to the Father on their behalf. I believe it strengthens one's faith to hear the actual prayer. That's why prayer is a *verbal* form of encouragement. In order for prayer to encourage, it must be heard.

2. Vocal prayer is encouraging because it reminds the person in need of support that he or she is not going it alone, but that a bigger Someone is in control. If I can grasp even one or two phrases of a friend's prayer for me, I can believe that God has some answers for my life that had previously been hidden to me.

3. An offer to pray is many times forgotten in the busyness of our lives if we don't stop to pray at the time we offer. It does little good to entertain the benevolent thought of praying for someone if we never get around to doing it. Just as it does little good to think good thoughts of others and say nothing.

Without verbal encouragement I would have given up a long time ago. I have been told that I'm a bad mom, and I thank God for those who have assured me otherwise. It makes me want to keep trying. Some have told me I am wasting my time writing. I hate to think about where I would be without those who have said, "You're doing great. Keep going."

Verbal encouragement makes me strong, so when verbal criticism raises its ugly head, it does not destroy me, but challenges me to be even stronger yet.

When God lays encouragement for someone on your heart, don't hesitate to give it. God's record for being on time and on target is perfect.

TIME TO CONSIDER

1. Do you ever call someone just to encourage that person? Have you ever prayed with that person on the phone?

2. Is your tone of voice one that encourages others? How can you put more of your heart into your words?

3. Do you find it necessary to give advice and feel bad when others don't take it? How can you offer suggestions instead of dole out advice?

4. How can you become more comfortable with your style so you don't have to mimic others? Think of three creative ways to encourage others, ways that are natural to you.

12

...

Physical Encouragement

The physical aspects of encouragement are for many people the most difficult to implement because these involve moving their bodies and oftentimes giving "everything" that they have and are. Fortunately, there are some altruistic and solicitous saints pledged to the body of Christ for whom serving and giving of themselves to others comes naturally. It is impossible for them *not* to give. What would we do without these special people?

For the most part, I would guess the majority of us do not fall into that category. Acts of giving and serving don't occur to us often, and when we are given the opportunity to encourage others in this way, we fumble around, wondering how to facilitate the process and sometimes completely talking ourselves out of it. This type of encouragement may mean a sacrifice of time, money, or material possessions. It is definitely a laying down of one's life for another person. In this age of the "me generation," giving is quite an unusual exploit.

Physical encouragement also includes the acts of touching, hand squeezing, and hugging. Unless it's a premarital back-seat-of-the-car experience, I doubt that anyone can receive "too much" affection. I'm naive enough to assume that if a person will touch me, that person must also love me. And don't we all need to be loved?

The physical part of encouragement is also necessary for us as encouragers. We need to be able to feel that we are contributing. Those who separate themselves from the hub of the Christian community never know the fulfillment that comes from the sense of others needing them and from being able to contribute something of value.

So, for those of us who are not inherent givers, servers, or touchers, the good news is we can learn how to function in these roles. We may not ever be completely adept in these areas, but we can be at ease enough to be able to help those who need us. Besides, when we are too comfortable, we can become complacent or arrogant. A little discomfort never hurt anyone.

THE NATURE OF GIVING

". . . the righteous give without sparing" (Prov. 21:26).

If anyone should, Christians should give all that they are to every person all of the time. Sound like a huge order? It is. Yet, this scripture exhorts us to give without sparing. Is that any less than all?

The word *sparing* here is a derivative of the Hebrew word *chasak,* meaning "to restrain, refrain, refuse, preserve, or withhold." What does that tell us? That we are to give freely, with no restraints, no holding back, no strings attached. Giving is so much more than physical action. It

136

is an attitude of the heart, which is where every good deed originates.

We progress naturally and rapidly through a variety of emotions when we see someone hurting. Here's a small sampling—not necessarily typical, but possible nonetheless:

1. "Oh . . . that poor person. That's really too bad." Some people's emotional response progresses no further, which really *is* "too bad."

2. "How awful. I hope someone helps."

3. "God, this person needs help. Will you please do something?" A lot of people quit right here because, having prayed, they feel as if they've done their part. Prayer, after observing a hurting person, pacifies the observer's uncomfortable feelings of uncertainty as to whether or not to get involved. Of course, those times do occur when we find the situation beyond our control. Then we really can do nothing but pray. However, those times may be fewer than we might like to admit.

4. "How can I help? What do I have to offer this hurting person?" This is the pivotal point where we can launch into action if we so choose. So much depends on how confident we feel to move into another person's need, how spiritually and emotionally strong we are at the moment, and whether we have gathered within our storehouse the resources to make the difference.

People's hurts are not always visible to the naked eye. We may have to look below the surface of their lives and listen closely when they talk. Recently I sympathized with a friend whose home was being foreclosed. During the course of the conversation, she mentioned her humiliation at the need to borrow money from friends or relatives each week to buy groceries.

I wanted to help. And though I couldn't stop foreclosure

of her house, I could buy food. But I wondered if I should buy the groceries and take them to her. I might not provide what she really needed. Should I give her the money instead? If I did she might be tempted to pay an outstanding bill. I ended up taking her to the store, telling her how much I wanted to give her, and letting her pick out her own groceries.

As it turned out, because of an unexpected expense of my own, I would not have been able to help her the following week. God allowed me to find out about my friend's need when I did, when I could help.

If you are being sensitive to those around you, you'll hear about needs all the time. The very hearing itself should alert you to the possibility that God may have set up the encounter because He wanted to use you to meet the other person's need—in which case you should feel honored He would trust you with such an undertaking.

We can learn from those who are natural-born givers. I know two women who live together on a farm, which in itself is a full-time job; yet they both have other full-time work and use every spare minute giving to others. I've seen them give of themselves bountifully in every category thus far mentioned. They give money (in large amounts) to those in financial need. They are on the spot with their tractor when they hear that someone needs a garden Rototilled. At times when my family has struggled financially, these dear givers, without any fanfare, have taken my children and outfitted them in whole new sets of clothes. They never asked me if we needed it. They simply knew—because they're so sensitive to others in this area. They are esteemed highly because of their encouraging and charitable acts of giving.

As I've watched them, I've learned much about giving and the attitude accompanying it. They love every minute of it and jump at every opportunity to share of themselves and their resources.

If a person hurts too long, his faith in God's caring begins to be shaken. Giving encourages because not only are the receiver's needs met, but the assurance that God still cares is reinforced.

SERVING

Serving others takes many forms. It can be anything from helping a friend move a houseful of furniture to caring for a sick mother's children or assisting a neighbor in replacing a roof.

Serving is an attitude of heart that says, "I want to help you. Thank you for allowing me the privilege of sharing what I have and who I am with you." The server moves confidently into a confusing situation and brings order. The server works behind the scenes meeting needs, performing the menial tasks of life, doing someone else's dirty work, caring not if credit is given. The true server's motive is to make life easier for others, to make less painful the hurts of the wounded, to clean up the messes of the discouraged so life can progress.

People serve one another for a variety of reasons. A maid may serve a family solely for the purpose of making a living. Jacob served Laban seven years (it turned out to be fourteen) for the hand of Rachel in marriage. Caddies may serve golfers for the valuable experience they gain from watching the pros.

The type of serving we are discussing here is for the purpose of encouraging. Since true service goes deeper than the actual act itself, since it evolved from somewhere inside us, how can we incorporate into our basic nature the server's heart?

Servers seem to see things other people miss. Sometimes

The Gift of Encouragement

I can walk into a roomful of people, and after a few moments of talking with them, I can fairly accurately sense the emotional, intellectual, and spiritual needs of the group. A server sees the physical needs and is constantly evaluating how to best meet those needs.

Joyce, a neighbor of mine, has suffered with cancer for over a year. When I visit her, I pray with her, I listen to her, and I try to help her cope emotionally. Fortunately, she has other friends, true servers, who see a house needing to be cleaned, children needing to be cared for, meals needing to be cooked. I have done some of those things for Joyce but you have to bodily position me somewhere in the house and point out a specific task. Otherwise, I just don't see it. I also feel awkward doing things in someone else's home. Yet, I don't feel the least bit uncomfortable when Joyce cries. Many people would much rather clean her house than watch her cry.

We're all different. We have different strengths and weaknesses. But while we use our natural abilities in our personal style, we can also concentrate on developing our weak areas, so that the Lord can use us in a much broader capacity.

A server doesn't wait to be asked. A server moves confidently into a situation and begins to serve. I appreciate anyone's willingness to serve. However, I see it as a real cop-out to say, "If there's anything I can do to help, let me know."

I have never yet responded to anyone who has said that to me. But when someone says to me, "I would like to watch your children next weekend so you can go to the beach," I hop up and down with glee and begin packing five little knapsacks.

My two friends on the farm did that very thing. They insisted on taking all five of my children, then sent me off to the beach. I'll be ever grateful for their thoughtfulness. They saw my need to get away and eagerly jumped in to meet it. If they had said, "If you ever need anything, let us know," I never would have answered, "Funny you should offer. As a matter of fact, I was thinking about going to the beach next weekend. Would you mind watching my five kids?"

I've noticed that most servers are embarrassed by lavish praise and thanks for their deeds. They would rather function incognito. Their fulfillment comes in meeting specific needs, rather than in the credit their receive for doing so.

Servers are encouragers in that:

1. They meet the needs of others that would never be met without them.

2. They provide a source of inspiration in their consistent unselfishness.

3. Their approach is one of humility.

4. They go above and beyond what is expected of them.

To be a server is to accept one of the highest callings in the body of Christ.

". . . whoever wants to become great among you must be your servant" (Matt. 20:26).

TOUCHING

I find it tragic in our day that most people seem to work very hard to keep as much distance between themselves and others as they possible can. In this age we have been conditioned to believe our biggest enemy is other people. From what we hear, see, and read in the electronic or written media, it seems that almost everyone is either crazy or on the edge of insanity. We have become caught up in survival, in protecting ourselves as much from our next-door neighbor as from nuclear weapons. With all of the crazies out in the world, our lives seem to be in as much danger when we walk out our front door as they are when an unknown finger is poised over a button that ultimately could blow our world into a billion pieces.

Jesus touched people wherever He went. As the Son of God, He possessed the power to heal without laying a hand on anyone. Yet, why did He touch them?

Why do you touch people? Or if you don't, why don't you? When others hug you or take your hand, do you respond positively or do you wait uncomfortably until they release you?

Based on our various backgrounds, hurts, or past relationships, many of us carry around all kinds of phobias rendering it almost impossible to relate naturally to others in the way God intended. I love you, but how to express that love is a constant struggle for me. I would like to hug you, but I don't know you well enough to know if I will offend you by doing so.

We must be careful not to invade other people's territory. Let them have as much distance as they need. *You* know you're a wonderful person, but you cannot convince other people without letting them see it for themselves in their own time and way.

Many of the people I once held at bay have bridged the gap and are now my dearest friends. A couple of them are huggers. In the past, I would have run from their physical expressions of encouragement, but now I look forward to it. Okay, I guess I have to admit that I, too, have the need to be loved, touched, embraced.

"There is a time for everything . . . a time to embrace and a time to refrain" (Eccles. 3:1, 5). As in everything we do, timing is an important factor in when to touch and when not to touch others. Sometimes the vibes you receive from others will scream at you, "Don't touch me!

142

Leave me alone!"—yet to be touched and held is exactly what they're crying out for. Others mean just what the vibes indicate—"stand clear." It does little good to reach out to them until they want you to.

I transmit vibes all the time that proclaim, "Leave me alone," when what I mean is, "Here I am. Love me. Even a pat on the head would be nice." Unfortunately, needs often go unmet either because the body language doesn't match one's true emotions or we do not know how to read each other, or we're not listening to the Holy Spirit as He makes us sensitive to the needs of others—no matter what they say they need or don't need.

Because some of us were raised by parents who rarely touched us or each other and because some of us are single, we especially need someone to reach out to us. Even a quick little squeeze can say, "Hey, you're okay. I like you." I can ride on that alone for a week.

When it comes to touching, we can relate in one of two ways—like a coiled-up rattlesnake ready to strike, or like a cuddly teddy bear ready to hug. If we assume the teddy-bear attitude, others will feel comfortable around us, whether or not we actually initiate the hug. For a teddy bear's stance is with arms wide open, anticipating his next exchange of love. How can we bear (I couldn't resist the pun) to disappoint him?

I love to love, and I love to be loved. In its simplest terms, a hug is an expression of love—certainly nothing to fear, but something to be experienced and savored.

Any form of physical encouragement, because of its tangibility, is as important to the health of the body of Christ as its spiritual and emotional counterparts. While Jesus lived on earth, He touched and served everywhere He went. In His death, He gave all—the Ultimate Servant.

The Gift of Encouragement

Giving, serving, touching—the very least we can offer is ourselves.

TIME TO CONSIDER

1. Why is a hug so encouraging? Do you feel comfortable hugging others or being hugged by others? Why or why not?

2. How can you as "the righteous give without sparing" (Prov. 21:26)? What are the gifts God has given you for encouraging others? How are you using them?

3. List three ways you enjoy serving others. Who needs you to serve them in any of these ways now?

4. Is it always encouraging to give, serve, and touch? When is it unwise to do these things? Can you discern the difference?

5. Why is it so important to wait on the Lord for His timing when it comes to using your gift?

6. When you encounter a hurting person, what is the first thing you feel like offering? Is it usually what's needed?

13
...

The Lifestyle Encourager

Encouragement is not merely an action we perform on occasion. Encouragement is a way of life, a lifestyle. It can become as much a part of us as eating and breathing. And how do we incorporate it into our lives? The same way we do any attribute—by doing and by being. This means that we perform actions and speak words that may at times make us uncomfortable. But we do them anyway because we care for others and want them to be all they can be. Encouragement happens in two ways. We either position ourselves in the right place at the right time to be able to help someone or it flows out of wherever we happen to be.

Ann Kiemel believes the world can only be changed one person at a time. For that reason she did not move into politics, the evangelism circuit, public education, or one of the many other bureaucratic systems to make her impact. Instead, she simply exemplifies life, encouragement, and ministry wherever she happens to be, whether on a plane or at a gas station. I doubt that anyone could argue the point that this young woman has made a significant difference in her world.

The development of certain personality traits and spiritual disciplines will help us to become lifestyle encouragers.

SPEND TIME IN GOD'S PRESENCE

To set aside a special time each day when we concentrate on nothing but the Lord Himself is essential for every Christian, but especially for the encourager. This is because the encourager is being drained whenever he or she is with people, and the necessary renewing and refreshing can only happen in the presence of God. Jesus withdrew from people often, not because He was anti-social, but because He was in need of being built up by the Father. Without this renewal, He would have less to give the people. If this was true for Jesus, how much more so for us mortals.

We know that God's presence does not come and go in our lives. We live in His presence always. However, when we consciously make room for Him and tune out everything and everybody else, we open ourselves up to hearing His voice more clearly. We listen to Him speak in a way not possible in the hustle and bustle of our daily lives. In the stillness of our souls, He will encourage us so we may in turn encourage others.

In the presence of God we cultivate a sense of who we are—not only to Him, but to ourselves and to others as well. We learn exactly what is our responsibility and what is not. We gain fresh perspective on yesterday, strength for today, and hope for tomorrow, which in turn can effect life-changing results in others as we touch their lives.

PRAY WITHOUT CEASING

In relating Paul's admonition to "pray without ceasing" specifically to the encourager, it becomes a matter of lifting up other's needs to the Lord in such a way that we're not just asking the Lord to help, heal, and minister. Instead, we're asking Him to show *us* how He wants to use *us* to bring about the desired healing in their lives.

Not only: "God, Dave has cancer. Please heal him." But also: "In the meantime, how do you want to use me to make life easier for him? What resources do I have at my disposal that I can make available to him?"

Not only: "God, Kathy is lonely. She needs a friend. Please bring someone to her." But also: "Am I that someone?"

When God asks us to do something or be somebody for others, He enables us to do or be what He asks. If we honestly don't want to get involved, we'd better not pray about it. However, if the desire to pray for another is already within your heart, the desire to care for that person is probably there, too. The problem arises when we pray and then don't bother to listen to God's response to our concern. That's one reason so many people's needs go unmet, even when the person standing right next to them holds an answer. The person standing there is not listening.

Much unnecessary hurting prevails within the church. When we pray without ceasing, we also need to listen without ceasing to the forthcoming answer.

BE AVAILABLE

When you place a classified ad in the local newspaper

147

for a service you're offering or an item you're selling, don't you usually plan to stay home as much as possible to answer the phone? Otherwise, why place the ad? It's impossible for anyone to answer the ad if you're not available.

One dictionary defines the word *available* as capable of being used; obtainable; reachable; handy or accessible. Are you handy or accessible? Or are you too tied up in busyness: rebating, soap operas, and the like?

Busyness isn't even all bad—if it involves people. Activities such as car-pooling or PTA in themselves provide strategic opportunities to encourage, if you're alert. But it's hard to encourage a coupon or a television set.

If, as an encourager, you want to make yourself available, how do you go about it? It's really quite simple. The encourager needs a caring heart and at least one other person. That means the encourager needs to be where other people are, involved in people activities.

If you happen to be a member of a health spa and find yourself there once or twice a week, make a conscious effort to connect with the other members. The natural inclination may be to keep to yourself whether at the spa or the store, on a bus, walking through a park, or in one of many other places. However, when we know our calling as encouragers and make ourselves available to our world, it becomes less a conscious effort and more a natural way of relating to others.

SEEK OUT OPPORTUNITIES

Whereas making ourselves available is somewhat of a passive stance, seeking out opportunities is an active one. We can set up encounters that may allow us the privilege of encouraging. Jesus made Himself available as He walked the streets of Galilee, and many people flocked to

Him. Yet, He also sought out certain others who He knew needed Him.

To seek an opportunity is to extend yourself for the express purpose of encouraging someone. When I began teaching my first Bible study, my friend, Sharon, relinquished one evening with her family each week to come and support and encourage me as a teacher.

Go where people need you. *Go* where people are hurting. *Go* to the weak, the vulnerable, the sick, the imprisoned. In the name of Jesus Christ, *go* to them so that they may be healed and set free. If you don't go, who will?

Some people do not even know they need encouragement because they have managed so completely to deny their pain. To be an encourager to such people may mean "pushing the buttons" that will cause the pain to surface and force them to deal with their suppressed emotions. When these individuals suddenly realize that they're not nearly as strong or as put together as they had previously thought, they will need encouragement more than ever. For that reason, lifestyle encouragers cannot go around pushing everyone's buttons unless they are prepared to stick around afterward to clean up the subsequent mess. Otherwise, the hurt has no place to go, no ongoing healing can happen, and the wound will fester. The pain will turn inward and often grow in intensity, becoming a phobia or neurosis.

So, when we push a button, it becomes our responsibility to then walk with that person through the ensuing pain to a place of healing. It may take hours, days, weeks, or months. It may even take years. In my own life, two dear friends have walked with me through six years of pain, wondering (I'm sure) whether we would ever see the healing. There were times when I didn't respond, times when I turned my back and apparently didn't care.

Still, they stayed—and not only stayed, but continued pressing gently on the painful areas, risking rejection, risking our very relationship.

And now, finally, after all these years together, we are seeing the completion of the mission of encouragement they took on themselves so long ago. They are releasing me a little at a time, watching me try my wings, standing close in case I falter.

Without having been touched by their lives, I wonder where I would be today. I shudder when I think about it. Likewise, I stand in awe as I watch the ministry that takes place in others' lives whenever I seek out opportunities to encourage.

RELAX—DON'T STRIVE

A lifestyle encourager is enveloped in an aura of peace. This fruit of the spirit must accompany us if we are to be effective in our encouraging.

People who overreact to others and who are quick to dole out advice are usually nervous individuals. They feel pressure to be always on the spot and ready with an answer to fix another's life. Before they even open their mouths, their uptight attitude negates any sage advice they might have to offer.

When someone begins to pour out his or her heart to you and you begin to sense that God wants you to encourage this person, the tendency to panic rises strong. What if you say the wrong thing? What if you cry? Worse yet, what if you say something stupid and the other person cries?

If it's any consolation, all of these things and more have happened to me as an encourager and also to those have encouraged me. But God somehow always manages to redeem the situation if we don't launch a boat on the river of our tears and furiously paddle away for fear of staying and making things worse.

My words to you are "Don't panic." If the right words fail to come immediately . . . wait. With little urging, a hurting person will usually continue to talk until you feel you have something to offer. Most often what you offer may be no more than:

"Tell me about it."

"I'm so sorry."

"How did that make you feel?"

"That must have been terrible."

"How can I help?"

You will want to assure that individual of your continued love and support, of his or her value to you and others as a person.

Jesus Christ was peace and relaxation personified. He was in no hurry to get to Lazarus's tomb. He "reclined" often. He exhorted Martha to relax. And even though I can picture Jesus running, it's never in a frenzy or panic, rather it's more like loping.

As you strive to be a lifestyle encourager, realize that the future of the world does not depend on your next words, although it may seem so at the time. The person you are is right for the situations in which God chooses to place you. Don't try to play the role of parent, psychologist, or pastor to those who confide in you.

Relax and be you. That's all anyone expects of you, anyway. Play the part the fits you best—yourself.

HANDLE OR LAY ASIDE YOUR OWN PROBLEMS

As we have already established, simply because we become encouragers of others does not make us immune to life's troubles. Encouragers may actually be more susceptible to life's difficulties because they are regularly being drained of their energy resources by others, leaving them sorely lacking at times to help themselves. Another reason is that because they are such a threat to the kingdom of darkness, they become key targets for Satan's aims.

For whatever the reason, our own problems and struggles abound. As encouragers, we must learn to handle them or lay them aside, however temporarily, for the purpose of encouraging others.

Not long ago I lay sick in bed for a week. My children were also sick. Not only was I suffering physically, but I was also feeling like a total failure in other areas of my life. The phone rang and a local church leader greeted me and invited me to speak to her woman's group on—guess what?—encouragement. I answered politely that I'd be more than happy to, hung up, and laughed. "God, if this is your idea of a joke, it's not funny," I screamed.

For the next few weeks I would mutter periodically, "This isn't fair. I don't have a choice. I have to get it together whether I like it or not."

And I did. My own problems didn't miraculously disappear. But because I take encouraging others so seriously, if I feel what I am going through will hinder them, I will do anything in my power to pull it together. In this case, I handled my internal attitudes about an external problem and laid the core aside until the meeting was over. Then I decided, since everything was moving along so nicely, I would make a stab at the core.

So placing ourselves in a position of encouraging others, no matter how we feel, can actually stimulate us to move through our own troubles at a quicker pace than we would otherwise.

Whether or not we can lay aside our personal concerns depends greatly on the nature of the problem itself. As I moved through my divorce, one of the most discouraging things to me was that I could seldom pull myself together long enough to encourage those who had previously depended on me for support. I felt awful about this, but I simply lacked the strength. I also felt guilty every time I received encouragement because I thought I didn't deserve to receive it if I couldn't give it.

Some problems are such heavy burdens that we can't just lightly toss them aside. It takes time to separate ourselves from them and to regain the strength to encourage others. For that reason it's important that we don't burden an already overburdened person with our own problems. We must learn how to lay ourselves down for others.

"BE" AN ENCOURAGER

You *are* an encourager. It is part of your identity, although you may not realize it. Jesus went about "doing good," not because He felt it was His duty as Son of God or because He wanted to be popular, but because *He was good*. He couldn't help but do good. Goodness evolved out of His very nature.

"We have the mind of Christ" (1 Cor. 2:16).

We are "partakers of the divine nature" (2 Pet. 1:4, KJV).

Was Jesus an encourager? Do we not have His mind and nature within us?

Through the Holy Spirit, all the attributes of the character of Jesus Christ are resident in us as believers. Meditate on the far-reaching implications of that.

Unfortunately these qualities do not simply flow out of the wonderful people we are. (Cough! Sputter!) Although they become available to us at the time of salvation, we must learn to activate them into our lives. As we make use of them on a regular basis, these attributes of goodness become a part of us. As you learn to encourage others, encouragement becomes a part of your nature. Just as juice squirts from an orange when it's squeezed, so will encouragement spring forth from you when you're prodded with others' needs.

Laura Archer Huxley advises us:

From the time of Hippocrates, every good doctor has understood the therapeutic value of confidence and hope, has known how dangerous it is for the sick to hear the wrong kind of words. And the wrong kind of words may be uttered with the best intentions.[1]

If the body of Christ would take seriously Paul's admonition to "encourage one another," I will boldly state that we would put many of today's physicians and psychiatrists out of business. Depression—which is so often caused by what we allow others to do or say about us—and its subsequent physical pains (ulcers, headaches, stomachaches) would significantly decrease if we could depend on one another for an uplift after a fall.

As we begin to lay down our lives for the purpose of encouraging others, the body of Christ will once again become the healthy, vibrant, pulsating organism described in the Book of Acts. Only a healthy, caring people can minister to a sick and hurting world.

It's a big step. Will you take my hand? We need each other.

Two are better than one,
    because they have a good return for their work:
If one falls down,
    his friend can help him up.
But pity the man who falls
    and has no one to help him up!

Also, if two lie down together, they will keep warm.
   But how can one keep warm alone?
Though one may be overpowered,
   two can defend themselves.
A cord of three strands is not quickly broken.

Ecclesiastes 4:9–12

TIME TO CONSIDER

1. How are you available to God? When He needs an encourager, do you have to clear your calendar or are you free enough to move on His nudging?

2. Are you looking for opportunities to encourage others? How should you change your lifestyle so that you're available to hurting people?

3. Do you panic when others hurt in front of you? What can you do to remind yourself that this person's problem is ultimately God's, that you can't solve it, and that you are only an expression of His love?

4. Are you praying for the people you're encouraging? How can you be more conscious of their needs in prayer without resorting to a formal list?

5. Do you long to be a lifestyle encourager? As you become more conscious of God's will for you in this area, how to you plan to make encouragement a part of your everyday life?

Source Notes

Chapter 6

1. *How to Be a People Helper* by Gary Collins, copyright © 1976 by Vision House, Santa Ana, CA. Used by permission.

2. John Powell, *Why Am I Afraid to Tell You Who I Am?* (Niles, IL: Argus Communications, 1969), 144.

3. Ibid, 117.

Chapter 7

1. Chuck Swindoll, *Improving Your Serve* (Waco, TX: Word Books, 1981), 175.

2. Ibid, 157.

Chapter 9

1. *How to Be a People Helper* by Gary Collins, copyright ©1976 by Vision House, Santa Ana, CA. Used by permission.

Chapter 10

1. Jeanne Doering, "The Power of Encouragement," *Christian Herald,* March 1983, 26.

Chapter 11

1. Laura Archer Huxley, *You Are Not the Target* (New York: Farrar, Straus and Giroux; 1963), 180, 181.
2. Ibid.

Chapter 13

1. Laura Archer Huxley, *You Are Not the Target* (New York: Farrar, Straus and Giroux, 1963), 180.

Support Group Leader's Guide

Issue-oriented, problem-wrestling, life-confronting—Heart Issue books are appropriate for adult Sunday school classes, individual study, and especially for support groups. Here are guidelines to encourage and facilitate support groups.

SUPPORT GROUP GUIDELINES

The small group setting offers individuals the opportunity to commit themselves to personal growth through mutual caring and support. This is especially true of Christian support groups, where from five to twelve individuals meet on a regular basis with a mature leader to share their personal experiences and struggles over a specific "heart issue." In such a group, individuals develop trust and accountability with each other and the Lord. Because a support group's purpose differs from a Bible study or prayer group, it needs its own format and guidelines.

Let's look at the ingredients of a support group:
- Purpose
- Leadership
- Meeting Format
- Group Guidelines

PURPOSE

The purpose of a Heart Issue support group is to provide:

1. An *opportunity* for participants to share openly and honestly their struggles and pain over a specific issue in a non-judgmental, Christ-centered framework.

2. A *"safe place"* where participants can gain perspective on a mutual problem and begin taking responsibility for their responses to their own situations.

3. An *atmosphere* that is compassionate, understanding, and committed to challenging participants from a biblical perspective.

Support groups are not counseling groups. Participants come to be supported, not fixed or changed. Yet, as genuine love and caring are exchanged, people begin to experience God's love and acceptance. As a result, change and healing take place.

The initiators of a support group need to be clear about its specific purpose. The following questions are examples of what to consider before starting a small group.

1. What type of group will this be? A personal growth group, a self-help group, or a group structured to focus on a certain theme? Is it long-term, short-term, or ongoing?

2. Who is the group for? A particular population? College students? Single women? Divorced people?

3. What are the goals for the group? What will members gain from it?

4. Who will lead or co-lead the group? What are his/her qualifications?

5. How many members should be in the group? Will new members be able to join the group once it is started?

6. What kind of structure or format will the group have?

7. What topics will be explored in the support book and to what degree will this be determined by the group members and to what degree by the leaders?

LEADERSHIP

Small group studies often rotate leadership among participants, but because support groups usually meet for a specific time period with a specific mutual issue, it works well to have one leader or a team of co-leaders responsible for the meetings.

Good leadership is essential for a healthy, balanced group. Qualifications include character and personality traits as well as life experience and, in some cases, professional experience.

Personal Leadership Characteristics

COURAGE

One of the most important traits of effective group leaders is courage. Courage is shown in willingness (1) to be open to self-disclosure, admitting their own mistakes and taking the same risks they expect others to take; (2) to confront another, and, in confronting, to understand that love is the goal; (3) to act on their beliefs and hunches; (4) to be emotionally touched by another and to draw on their experiences in order to identify with the other; (5) to continually examine their inner self; (6) to be direct and honest with members; and (7) to express to the group their fears and expectations about the group process. (Leaders shouldn't use their role to protect themselves from honest

161

and direct interaction with the rest of the group.)
WILLINGNESS TO MODEL

Through their behavior, and the attitudes conveyed by it, leaders can create a climate of openness, seriousness of purpose, acceptance of others, and the desirability of taking risks. Group leaders should have had some moderate victory in their own struggles, with adequate healing having taken place. They recognize their own woundedness and see themselves as persons in process as well. Group leaders lead largely by example—by doing what they expect members to do.
PRESENCE

Group leaders need to be emotionally present with the group members. This means being touched by others' pain, struggles, and joys. Leaders can become more emotionally involved with others by paying close attention to their own reactions and by permitting these reactions to become intense. Fully experiencing emotions gives leaders the ability to be compassionate and empathetic with their members. At the same time, group leaders understand their role as facilitators. They know they're not answer people; they don't take responsibility for change in others.
GOODWILL AND CARING

A sincere interest in the welfare of the others is essential in group leaders. Caring involves respecting, trusting, and valuing people. Not every member is easy to care for, but leaders should at least want to care. It is vital that leaders become aware of the kinds of people they care for easily and the kinds they find it difficult to care for. They can gain this awareness by openly exploring their reactions to members. Genuine caring must be demonstrated; merely saying so is not enough.

Some ways to express a caring attitude are: (1) inviting

a person to participate but allowing that person to decide how far to go; (2) giving warmth, concern, and support when, and only when it is genuinely felt; (3) gently confronting the person when there are obvious discrepancies between a person's words and her behavior; and (4) encouraging people to be what they could be without their masks and shields. This kind of caring requires a commitment to love and a sensitivity to the Holy Spirit.

OPENNESS

To be effective, group leaders must be open with themselves, open to others in groups, open to new experiences, and open to life-styles and values that differ from their own. Openness is an attitude. It doesn't mean that leaders reveal every aspect of their personal lives; it means that they reveal enough of themselves to give the participants a sense of person.

Leader openness tends to foster a spirit of openness within the group; it permits members to become more open about their feelings and beliefs; and it lends a certain fluidity to the group process. Self-revelation should not be manipulated as a technique. However, self-evaluation is best done spontaneously, when appropriate.

NONDEFENSIVENESS

Dealing frankly with criticism is related closely to openness. If group leaders are easily threatened, insecure in their work of leading, overly sensitive to negative feedback, and depend highly on group approval, they will probably encounter major problems in trying to carry out their leadership role. Members sometimes accuse leaders of not caring enough, of being selective in their caring, of structuring the sessions too much, of not providing enough direction, of being too harsh. Some criticism may be fair, some unfair. The crucial thing for leaders is to nondefensively explore with their groups the feelings that are legitimately produced by the leaders and those that represent what is upsetting the member.

STRONG SENSE OF SELF

A strong sense of self (or personal power) is an important quality of leaders. This doesn't mean that leaders would manipulate or dominate; it means that leaders are confident of who they are and what they are about. Groups "catch" this and feel the leaders know what they are doing. Leaders who have a strong sense of self recognize their weaknesses and don't expend energy concealing them from others. Their vulnerability becomes their strength as leaders. Such leaders can accept credit where it's due, and at the same time encourage members to accept credit for their own growth.

STAMINA

Group leading can be taxing and draining as well as exciting and energizing. Leaders need physical and emotional stamina and the ability to withstand pressure in order to remain vitalized until the group sessions end. If leaders give in to fatigue when the group bogs down, becomes resistive, or when members drop out, the effectiveness of the whole group could suffer. Leaders must be aware of their own energy level, have outside sources of spiritual and emotional nourishment, and have realistic expectations for the group's progress.

SENSE OF HUMOR

The leaders who enjoy humor and can incorporate it appropriately into the group will bring a valuable asset to the meetings. Sometimes humor surfaces as an escape from healthy confrontations and sensitive leaders need to identify and help the group avoid this diversion. But because we often take ourselves and our problems so seriously, we need the release of humor to bring balance and perspective. This is particularly true after sustained periods of dealing seriously with intensive problems.

CREATIVITY

The capacity to be spontaneously creative, to approach each group session with fresh ideas is a most important characteristic for group leaders. Leaders who are good at discovering new ways of approaching a group and who are willing to suspend the use of established techniques are unlikely to grow stale. Working with interesting co-leaders is another way for leaders to acquire fresh ideas.

GROUP LEADERSHIP SKILLS

Although personality characteristics of the group leader are extremely significant, by themselves they do not ensure a healthy group. Leadership skills are also essential. The following need to be expressed in a sensitive and timely way:

ACTIVE LISTENING

Leaders need to absorb content, note gestures, observe subtle changes in voice or expression, and sense underlying messages. For example, a woman may be talking about her warm and loving feelings toward her husband, yet her body may be rigid and her fists clenched.

EMPATHY

This requires sensing the subjective world of the participant. Group leaders, in addition to being caring and open, must learn to grasp another's experience and at the same time maintain their separateness.

RESPECT AND POSITIVE REGARD

In giving support, leaders need to draw on the positive assets of the members. Where differences occur, there needs to be open and honest appreciation and toleration.

WARMTH

Smiling has been shown to be especially important in the communication of warmth. Other nonverbal means are: voice tone, posture, body language, and facial expression.

GENUINENESS

Leaders need to be real, to be themselves in relating with others, to be authentic and spontaneous.

FORMAT

The format of meetings will differ vastly from group to group, but the following are generally accepted as working well with support groups.

MEETING PLACE

This should be a comfortable, warm atmosphere. Participants need to feel welcome and that they've come to a "safe place" where they won't be overheard or easily distracted. Some groups will want to provide baby-sitting.

OPENING

Welcome participants. The leader should introduce herself and the members should also introduce themselves. It is wise to go over the "ground rules" at every meeting and especially at first or when there are newcomers. Some of these would include:

1. Respect others' sharing by keeping what is said in the group confidential.

2. Never belittle the beliefs or expressions of another.

3. Respect the time schedule. Try to arrive on time and be prompt in leaving.

4. Feel free to contact the leader at another time if there are questions or need for additional help.

Many meetings open with a brief time of prayer and worship and conclude with prayer. It often helps to ask for informal prayer requests and brief sharing so that the group begins in a spirit of openness.

MEETING

Leaders can initiate the meeting by focusing on a

particular issue (or chapter if the group is studying a book). It is wise to define the focus of the specific meeting so that the group can stay on track for the entire session. (See Group Guidelines below.)

CLOSING

Strive for promptness without being abrupt. Give opportunity for those who need additional help to make an appointment with the leader. Be alert to any needing special affirmation or encouragement as they leave.

GROUP GUIDELINES

Because this is a support group, not an advice group, the leader will need to establish the atmosphere and show by her style how to relate lovingly and helpfully within the group. Participants need to know the guidelines for being a member of the group. It is a wise practice to repeat these guidelines at each meeting and especially when newcomers attend. The following guidelines have proven to be helpful to share with support groups:

1. You have come to give and receive support. No "fixing." We are to listen, support, and be supported by one another—not give advice.

2. Let other members talk. Please let them finish without interruption.

3. Try to step over any fear of sharing in the group. Yet do not monopolize the group's time.

4. Be interested in what someone else is sharing. Listen with your heart. Never converse privately with someone else while another member is addressing the group.

5. Be committed to express your feelings from the heart. Encourage others to do the same. It's all right to feel angry, to laugh, or to cry.

6. Help others own their feelings and take responsibility for change in their lives. Don't jump in with an easy

167

answer or a story on how you conquered their problem. Relate to where they are.

7. Avoid accusing or blaming. Speak in the "I" mode about how something or someone made *you* feel. Example: "I felt angry when. . . ."

8. Avoid ill-timed humor to lighten emotionally charged times. Let participants work through their sharing even if it is hard.

9. Keep names and sharing of other group members confidential.

10. Because we are all in various stages of growth, please give newcomers permission to be new and old-timers permission to be further along in their growth. This is a "safe place" for all to grow and share their lives.